GREAT
EXPECTATIONS

GREAT EXPECTATIONS

(THE LOST **TORONTO BLUE JAYS** SEASON)

SHI DAVIDI
JOHN LOTT

ecw press

Published by ECW Press
2120 Queen Street East, Suite 200,
Toronto, Ontario, Canada M4E 1E2
416-694-3348 / info@ecwpress.com

LIBRARY AND ARCHIVES CANADA
CATALOGUING IN PUBLICATION

Davidi, Shi, 1975–, author
Great expectations : the Lost Toronto Blue Jays Season
/ Shi Davidi, John Lott.

ISBN 978-1-77041-187-6 (pbk.)
ALSO ISSUED AS: 978-1-77090-423-1 (PDF)
978-1-77090-424-8 (ePUB)

1. Toronto Blue Jays (Baseball team). I. Lott, John,
1944–, author
II. Title.

GV875.T6D37 2013
796.357'6409713541   C2013-902460-3

Editors for the press: Jack David and Laura Pastore
Text design and colour insert: Tania Craan
Cover design and typesetting: Troy Cunningham
Cover images: (top) Frank Gunn/The Canadian
Press; (bottom) Tim Larson/Icon SMI
Back cover image: John Lott
Printing: Friesens 5 4 3 2 1

The publication of *Great Expectations* has been generously supported by the Ontario Arts Council
(OAC), an agency of the Government of Ontario, which last year funded 1,681 individual artists
and 1,125 organizations in 216 communities across Ontario for a total of $52.8 million. We also
acknowledge the financial support of the Government of Canada through the Canada Book Fund
for our publishing activities, and the contribution of the Government of Ontario through the Ontario
Book Publishing Tax Credit and the Ontario Media Development Corporation.

PRINTED AND BOUND IN CANADA

MIX
Paper from
responsible sources
FSC
www.fsc.org   FSC® C016245

To my sons Adyn and Zev, whose boundless energy will serve them well once they find their own field of dreams, and my wife Stacey, who continuously inspires me to keep striving on mine.

—Shi

To John Reindollar, my uncle, who handed me a baseball and taught me to play; to Joan Thomas, my grade 10 English teacher, who said my essay on Ted Williams reminded her of journalism; and to Nancy, for everything.

—John

"How my great expectations had all dissolved, like our own marsh mists before the sun, I could not understand."

—*Charles Dickens,*
Great Expectations

PROLOGUE

THRILLED. The word fairly flew from the tongue of Alex Anthopoulos. A reporter had just asked the Toronto Blue Jays' general manager how he felt about the performance of his manager, John Farrell, who, on this day in mid-August 2012, clung to the whirling tiller of a sinking ship. Before the question was fully formed, Anthopoulos spat a one-syllable vote of confidence.

Thrilled.

That was a stretch, and Anthopoulos knew it. Especially now, as rumours out of Boston claimed the Red Sox coveted Farrell to replace the pratfall-prone Bobby Valentine as their manager. Reportedly, Farrell was eager to oblige, not that he was about to say so in public. Earlier in the day, Farrell had cut short the daily media scrum in his office after a reporter asked about the Boston buzz. "I'm not going to comment on speculation or conjecture," he said testily before halting the session four minutes after it started.

Two and a half hours later, just before game time at the Rogers Centre, several reporters cornered Anthopoulos in the media dining room behind the press box and asked him about the Boston rumours. The 36-year-old general manager has an amiable way with the media, but he was starting to feel ambushed, in more ways than one.

Echoing Farrell, he refused to comment on rumours. Club policy is clear, Anthopoulos said: a contract employee may join a rival team only if the new job represents a promotion. Smug Red Sox fans probably figured a move from Toronto to Boston should qualify; after all, Farrell had gone to a foreign country to do his apprenticeship with an inferior club. It was only right that he return in triumph to Boston, where he had been a popular pitching coach for a storied franchise, to assume one of baseball's iconic jobs. Never mind that he had a year left on his Toronto contract.

No, Anthopoulos was *not* thrilled. He had begun to feel a vague sense of unease toward Farrell back in the spring, and with more than a month left in a season of perpetual torment, he did not need a public debate on the loyalty of his manager.

Absent from the playoffs for nearly two decades, the Blue Jays had entered the 2012 season on a familiar breeze of false hope. Within two months they were riding the cliff's edge, although the division race was tight and they remained in playoff contention, at least in a nominal sense. Then came an improbable plague of injuries that crippled the club in June and July.

By season's end, six pitchers had undergone elbow or shoulder surgery and another needed an operation to fix a broken foot. On July 16 in Yankee Stadium, slugger Jose Bautista wrecked his wrist while taking a swing that appeared innocuous, at least by his severe standards. Surgery subsequently ended his season. Two days later in the same venue, Canadian dynamo Brett Lawrie tried to run through an iron railing in pursuit of a foul ball and fell seven feet into a camera bay. Shortly thereafter, he missed a month with a muscle strain in his side. Capping a star-crossed July, a foul ball broke the hand of catcher J.P. Arencibia. He was out for six weeks.

Thin to begin with, the team was a virtual skeleton. But behind the scenes, Anthopoulos and Farrell surveyed the same scene and drew different conclusions, as they often had throughout the season.

As early as spring training, Anthopoulos felt his comfort level with Farrell start to slip, almost imperceptibly at first, when Farrell privately expressed doubts that the Blue Jays had the pitching depth they needed to contend in the American League East. Tension arose again as the July

31 trade deadline approached. Although the Blue Jays' record was 51-52 on that date, they were also five games away from a playoff berth. A long shot, to be sure, but with 59 games left, a shot worth taking, at least in the manager's view. Farrell prodded his GM to make a bold move or two to improve the team, but Anthopoulos stood pat, unable to find a deal he considered sensible for the long term. The manager was annoyed; so were some of his players. Farrell felt compelled to convene a clubhouse meeting in a bid to defuse the dissatisfaction. Anthopoulos offered to address the troops as well, but Farrell said, "I'll handle it."

Then in September, with the team battling Boston for last place, shortstop Yunel Escobar added insult to the injury epidemic. Before a Saturday game at the Rogers Centre, he scrawled three Spanish words on his eye black and became an overnight poster boy for homophobia after a fan took his picture and posted it online. The story broke as the Jays landed in New York for a series against the Yankees. In a hastily arranged news conference, Escobar apologized and said he had learned a lesson. He also said he meant no harm; after all, the offending word — *maricon*, loosely translated as "faggot" — is commonly, innocently, and jokingly used among Latin players, he said. In the clubhouse, several teammates backed him up. "It's just a word we use on an everyday basis," said Omar Vizquel. "I don't know why people are taking this so hard."

The team suspended Escobar for three games and ordered sensitivity training, but there was no graceful escape from this unseemly mess. Flanking their shortstop at the news conference, Anthopoulos and Farrell listened uncomfortably to Escobar's ambiguous *mea culpa*. When they spoke, they tried gamely to walk a narrow path that led inevitably into quicksand. They said they understood Escobar did not mean to offend, but condemned his behaviour as tactless and stupid. Their message lost some of its edge when several prominent Blue Jays — including Bautista and Edwin Encarnacion — chalked up the controversy to cross-cultural confusion.

Many observers were incredulous that Farrell and his coaching staff did not spot the message on Escobar's eye black before he took the field. If they didn't know what it meant, they should have, according to one rival manager. "That's a very common word around clubhouses. It should never have gotten out of the dugout," he says.

Anthopoulos and Farrell pride themselves on attention to detail and meticulous management of the message. They don't like surprises. The Escobar controversy blindsided them and undermined the myth that sports teams take pains to foster: through thick and thin, everyone is on the same page, pulling in the same direction.

Behind the scenes, the GM and his manager were pulling in different directions on another matter. With the season lost and Escobar disgraced, Farrell wanted to put prospect Adeiny Hechavarria in the lineup every day, preparing him for possible daily duty in 2013. Anthopoulos said no. Rival scouts had seen just enough of Hechavarria during a late-season call-up, he reasoned. Let the tease run into the off-season. In the right trade, Hechavarria could become a vital chip. No sense giving him a chance to diminish his value.

With a 73-89 season mercifully put to bed, one piece of nasty business remained. During a year-end review meeting, Anthopoulos put the question to Farrell: if Boston calls, do you want to go? Farrell said yes. Managing Boston was his "dream job," he said. Had Anthopoulos consented, he would have gone a year earlier. He insisted he had not neglected his responsibilities to the Blue Jays, but yes, he would jump at the chance to manage the Red Sox.

On cue, Boston called the next day. Anthopoulos quickly traded his manager for a backup infielder. Among many Toronto fans, the awkward divorce represented the final straw. In social media and on call-in shows, a simplistic but powerful narrative took root: Farrell's leaving was an act of betrayal. With his heart in Boston for at least a full year, he could not have given his best to the Blue Jays. And when he wanted out of his contract to join a division rival, Anthopoulos accommodated him, receiving little in return. It was embarrassing.

The playoffs were baseball's big October story, but the Blue Jays were becoming a sidebar about a team in disarray. As the game put its best foot forward, Toronto stubbed its toe.

By now, the exasperation of the fans had spread to the front office. The Blue Jays stood at a crossroads. Over his three years as general manager, Anthopoulos had been largely successful in selling a philosophy of patience and prudence. We will build the nucleus of a winner from our farm system, he said, then top up the team with a couple of prime free agents. A perpetual parade of prospects would sustain a contender for years to come. But the 2012 season had exposed the flaw in that plan. Depending on so many young players left the Jays short on depth, vulnerable to inevitable growing pains as well as unpredictable injuries. Year after year, the team's margin of error was too small. So was its payroll.

The Blue Jays needed a radical makeover. Their fertile farm system would help to make it happen. The change would come faster than anyone — including the general manager — could ever have imagined. Very soon, as he introduced an array of new Blue Jays to the city, Anthopoulos would use one of his favourite words again and again.

Thrilled.

THE BLOCKBUSTER | 1

"*Hopefully by the end of 2013, we'll say 2012 is the best year the organization had. We needed it for all these things to happen. And if that isn't the case, we'll just say that was a terrible year and we lived through it.*"

— Alex Anthopoulos in February 2013

BY THE TIME THE BLUE JAYS ended their 2012 season on October 3 at 73-89 after a 2-1 victory over the Minnesota Twins, all Alex Anthopoulos wanted to do was get away. In previous years the tireless GM immediately pushed himself and his lieutenants into post-mortem meetings that lasted for days, using those talks as a springboard into the winter's business, everything happening at a dizzying, manic pace. But all the losing in a year of misery, all the grinding of moving players up and down from the minors while scanning the waiver wire or working the phones to try to find some upgrades, had taken a toll on the whole organization. So Anthopoulos did something almost unthinkable for him — he told everyone to go home and take a break. Even the man known for sending 2 a.m. emails briefly stepped aside from work, returning home to Montreal to reconnect with family and celebrate Thanksgiving. He needed the time not only to get away from baseball, but also to relax with his immediate family and newborn son John, an August addition to his clan.

By the time the holiday weekend was over, he was ready to begin picking up the pieces of his baseball team, and the first order of business was debriefing manager John Farrell.

They spoke all day the Monday after Thanksgiving and again on Tuesday, exchanging information and ideas in an open, direct, and forthright manner they hadn't enjoyed for months. The conversations were mostly constructive, although there were tense moments. Farrell complained of instances when he felt Anthopoulos made decisions without considering his input. Anthopoulos countered by telling Farrell that he needed to be stronger in stating his case when something was especially important to him, and he shouldn't relent if he didn't believe in a particular move. Then, at the very end, Anthopoulos finally broached the subject they had stayed away from, but ultimately the one most pressing: what to make of all those clandestine feelers from the Boston Red Sox?

Anthopoulos raised the matter first, asking Farrell directly what he should do if the Red Sox called again, inquiring about his availability. Farrell replied by saying that if he had an opportunity to pursue the job, he'd be interested, the same response he gave nearly a year earlier when the Red Sox took their first run at him. The Blue Jays angrily rebuffed that effort by demanding frontline pitcher Clay Buchholz in return for their manager, abruptly ending the conversation. This time, Anthopoulos told Farrell the Blue Jays hadn't been contacted yet by their division rival, and that nothing could happen unless they were. Essentially, it was a message that the Blue Jays were ready to discuss trading him, a marked shift from the GM's public pronouncements that "John is our manager." They were done fighting for someone who wanted to be somewhere else.

The next day Red Sox owner John Henry called Blue Jays president Paul Beeston to ask about Farrell again, and the ball got rolling. Negotiations were primarily handled between Beeston and close friend Larry Lucchino, Red Sox president and CEO, with input on trade pieces from Anthopoulos and his Boston counterpart, Ben Cherington. For a deal to happen, the Blue Jays insisted they get a big-league player in return; their asks included Jacoby Ellsbury and top pitching prospect Rubby De La Rosa. The Red Sox started by offering Chris Carpenter, the right-hander they received from the Chicago Cubs a year earlier as compensation for former GM Theo Epstein. Over the next week and a half they went back and forth until October 20, when they finally settled on infielder Mike Aviles, the Blue Jays then granting the Red Sox permission to negotiate a new contract with Farrell. It was done that night; the Red Sox leaked word shortly before midnight (infuriating the Blue Jays), and an official announcement came the next day. "I'm extremely excited to be returning to the Red Sox and to Boston," Farrell said in a release issued by the Red Sox. "I love this organization."

While that irritated many Toronto fans, what twisted the knife was the news conference at Fenway Park on October 23, when Farrell was feted like a conquering hero back to reclaim a throne that was rightfully his. As he revelled in the moment, several Blue Jays players and staff felt that he made his time in Toronto seem like an internship. Some were irked that he finally got what he wanted, others were simply happy to see him go, while many were turned off by a commitment they had long questioned because of Farrell's public statements that never definitively dismissed the possibility of returning to Boston. The Toronto front office was furious and dumbfounded that he volunteered the information that he asked out of his deal in October 2011, a move that led the Blue Jays to institute a policy preventing their employees from breaking contracts for lateral moves. And worst of all was the way getting jilted by Farrell after two mediocre seasons of work sent the franchise boring through bedrock to a new low, while a division rival that had schemed and plotted for a year at last got their man, saddling the Blue Jays with a manager search they didn't necessarily want.

"It's over, it's finished. He's still in the game, we're still in the game," Beeston says tersely of the whole affair, his reluctance to discuss it underlining how touchy the matter remains. "I know what it was, Alex knows what it was, John Farrell knows what it was, Larry Lucchino knows what it was, John Henry knows what it was. That's good enough. It's done. We wish him good luck." Blue Jays fans were nowhere near as gracious, enraged by the doom and gloom Farrell left behind. But it was a decision the team had to make. "Do you really want somebody who doesn't want to be there, or wants to be somewhere else, in your organization?" says Keith Pelley, the head of Rogers Media. "What does that do for the culture, what does that do for the messaging to the players, and if you're not all in, and you don't have the unwavering passion, how successful are you going to be? So I think the decision they made with John was the right decision. It might have been a little bit different if we hadn't had 73 wins [in 2012], you know? We were 73-89 and had some challenges that were made public in the clubhouse. Things might have been different if it was the other way around and we were two games from a playoff position."

On the day of Farrell's departure, Anthopoulos said there were "zero" frontrunners in the search for a replacement, and he meant it. His mind was focused elsewhere.

WHILE FARRELL'S MESSY EXIT was being orchestrated, the plans for an off-season roster makeover were being mapped out on a series of whiteboards in luxury suites 327 and 328, which had been converted into a war room.

Interns were tasked with making magnets displaying the names of players on every big-league club, which were subsequently ranked by Anthopoulos, assistant general managers Tony LaCava, Jay Sartori, and Andrew Tinnish, and pro scouting director Perry Minasian. They slotted free agents by position for both the fall of 2012 and 2013, to give them a better sense of possible targets for the next year, and then began building scenarios of how to attack the winter, factoring in who might be available, how much they might cost, and how best to allocate the dollars.

Team owner Rogers Communications Inc. had already approved a payroll increase of roughly $20 million to $105 million before the season ended. Given the prior commitments the Blue Jays had in place of about $80 million, Anthopoulos had roughly $25 million to pursue an aggressive plan that included, in order of priority, two starting pitchers, an infielder, a reliever, and a left fielder. That's an ambitious shopping list on a limited budget, and the tight constraints meant Anthopoulos and his staff refined their past processes, narrowing the net they cast. With free agents, they pared down their list based on how a player would fit into both the payroll and the clubhouse, and what their potential alternatives were. In terms of trades, they locked in on players that teams would be motivated to move, rather than trying to be creative in search of players under long-term control. "It was like, we're not going to chase our tails and really try to go after a player that's going to be hard to pry," says Anthopoulos. "You might do it, but it's going to take so much time and effort, and we need to get a lot done, so let's be decisive and really key in on teams that, just from past knowledge, they'll be open to talking about this player and that player. Let's spend time talking about that."

To that end, as the San Francisco Giants were putting the finishing touches on a four-game sweep of the Detroit Tigers in the World Series, Anthopoulos was on the phone with the Chicago White Sox, trying to find out their plans for Jake Peavy. The 2007 National League Cy Young Award winner had a $22 million option for 2013 that was sure to be declined in favour of a $4 million buyout. Rick Hahn was on the verge of being named the new general manager and it was unclear which direction the club was heading, and whether negotiations on a new deal for Peavy would pan out. So the Blue Jays made sure to ask the White Sox to check in with them first before they declined Peavy's option and sent him into free agency. They also explored a trade for Dan Haren, whose $15.5 million option was going to be declined by the Los Angeles Angels, although they were wary about his health.

Meanwhile, the Blue Jays were also keeping a close eye on Tigers starter Anibal Sanchez, who was due to hit free agency once the Fall Classic ended. Of all the pitchers entering the open market, he was the one the Blue Jays focused in on, especially with Zack Greinke, an arm Anthopoulos had long coveted, demanding more than the five-year max they could offer under team policy. (The Los Angeles Dodgers eventually gave him $147 million over six years.) By the time Sergio Romo got Miguel Cabrera looking at a third strike to clinch the Giants' second title in three years on October 28, the Blue Jays were ready to pounce on multiple fronts.

One of the first places Anthopoulos landed was at the White Sox's door. Word was that talks with Peavy on a new deal weren't making much progress. The Blue Jays were willing to pick up his pricy option for 2013 and were ready to part with some prospects to make it happen. Dealing him away wasn't the White Sox's preference, but Hahn did the responsible thing and examined all options, and worked out a couple of different trade scenarios with Anthopoulos that he put on the back burner. The scenario the Blue Jays preferred had the White Sox absorbing the $4 million in buyout money they were going to pay anyway, making Peavy an $18 million budgetary hit, but that was still going to drain too much of their available payroll. So Anthopoulos and Beeston went to the ownership at Rogers Communications Inc., and during a meeting with CEO Nadir Mohamed, CFO Tony Staffieri, and Rogers Media head Keith Pelley, made a pitch for a one-time commitment over and above the already settled budget. They got it. "We sat around the board table and talked about Jake Peavy for about 90 minutes, a couple of hours, and at the end of the day, it was 'Alex, if you feel the Jake Peavy deal is what you need to do . . .'" recalls Pelley. "That was a pretty important conversation. That opened the door to 'we're ready to commit to spend more dollars.'"

In the interim, the White Sox closed in on a new contract with Peavy, whose preference was to stay in Chicago. He had been aware of the potential for a trade to another team, but not the specifics. On October 30, word leaked of a $29 million, two-year extension and its announcement came the next day, just ahead of the deadline for decisions on player options. The Peavy deal was dead. But ownership's willingness to ante up for it emboldened Anthopoulos as he turned to his next targets.

AS THE GENERAL MANAGERS' meetings loomed, the Blue Jays were juggling several balls, and first settled some smaller pieces of business. Mike Aviles, a member of the team for all of two weeks, and catcher Yan Gomes were shipped to the Cleveland Indians on November 3 for Esmil Rogers, a power-armed right-hander with four years of club control set to earn $509,000 in 2013. The trade was both surprising and understandable, as Anthopoulos appeared to have plugged a hole at second base with Aviles, but needed inexpensive relief help and found it in Rogers. And Anthopoulos by that point was deep in negotiations with Maicer Izturis, a utility infielder the Blue Jays felt would be an upgrade on Aviles. His $10 million, three-year contract would be signed just as baseball's movers and shakers arrived to do business at the desert oasis of Indian Wells, California.

Yet before checking into the Hyatt Regency Indian Wells Resort & Spa for two and a half days of meetings, Anthopoulos and assistant GM Tony LaCava also made a clandestine side trip to Miami on a much bigger play, intent on making a quick strike for Anibal Sanchez. Working through their various scenarios in the war room, the Blue Jays decided that of all the free-agent arms, Sanchez was the best they were likely to land, and sought to knock out their competition by getting something done early. Another of their prime targets, right-hander Hisashi Iwakuma, was already off the board, having re-signed with the Seattle Mariners on November 2 without really testing the market, so that added some urgency to the recruiting trip.

Things went well the first day, when Anthopoulos and LaCava took Sanchez and his wife out to dinner, and again the following afternoon when the same foursome lunched along with the pitcher's parents and grandparents. Afterward, Anthopoulos spoke with Gene Mato, Sanchez's agent, and asked, "Can we get this done early? We're going to be aggressive." The Blue Jays offered a five-year deal out of the gate but didn't mention the dollar figure — $75 million — they had in mind. First, they wanted to hear what Mato was thinking, and he replied by saying they were looking for an eight-year commitment, perhaps seven, a total non-starter either way. Sanchez and his wife also needed to visit Toronto to see what the city had to offer before making a decision, a reasonable request but one that would delay the process. According to Anthopoulos, the final message was "We're going to need a little time, we're going to have to talk to other teams, go through the process, get information." Anthopoulos also understood the process would involve multiple teams and likely drag into December. (He was right; Sanchez re-signed with the Tigers for $80 million over five years on December 17.) He and LaCava left for Indian Wells with Sanchez on the back burner, determined to dig up the pitching help they needed somewhere else.

Shortly after they landed at LAX and hopped into a rental SUV bound for Palm Springs, Anthopoulos called Miami Marlins president

Larry Beinfest and asked if they could schedule a meeting to discuss Josh Johnson, the strapping 6-foot-7 right-hander due to be a free agent at the end of 2013. The two had discussed Johnson the previous July, when the Blue Jays also inquired about Jose Reyes and Mark Buehrle. Those talks went nowhere, but things were different this time, as the Marlins planned to shed payroll after a failed build-up the previous off-season. They had already purged Hanley Ramirez, Omar Infante, and Sanchez the previous summer, and the Blue Jays believed they were ready to extend the off-load. Beinfest told Anthopoulos that he'd carve out some time in the next day or two.

When Anthopoulos and LaCava arrived at the luxurious resort, their suite was ready for business. Assistant GMs Jay Sartori and Andrew Tinnish and pro scouting director Perry Minasian had already set up computers, a projector, and easel pads so they could easily access stats, watch scouting video, and draft notes for all to discuss. The extra hands were in contrast to the way Anthopoulos handled his first three GM meetings as the man in charge, when only LaCava came along. The larger contingent would come in handy in the days ahead.

The meetings opened Wednesday, November 7, and Anthopoulos was as prepared as he'd ever been. Beinfest was one of a small handful of GMs on his mental must-chat-with list, but in his pocket were 30 laminated cheat sheets, each the size of a credit card, with targeted players from each big-league club listed on the front and back. "If you're at an event or something, and I may know that I'm talking to Atlanta and there's this one player we want to get, but there may be something further down the line that's not a target but is a player we might think is undervalued or we'd like to get put in a deal, and it's just a bit of a reminder," he explains in his typical rambling manner. "It may be a reliever that's out of options, this player is blocked . . . let's ask about him, too. When you're having a conversation, just throw him in there."

When Anthopoulos ran into Marlins general manager Mike Hill at one of the opening-day sessions — during which GMs pass notes to one another and type out texts under tables like lovestruck high-schoolers — he didn't need to reference his cards. He asked about speedy utility-man Emilio Bonifacio, as he had on countless other occasions, and Hill said his group was open to anything. Anthopoulos sent Beinfest a text about scheduling a meeting. He suggested 3 p.m. Thursday, in the Marlins suite. "Can I bring my guys?" asked Anthopoulos. "No problem" was the reply.

En route to the meeting the next afternoon, the Blue Jays crew ran into a group of Boston Red Sox executives and exchanged pleasantries. "We're thinking, 'They probably just came out from the Marlins suite, too,'" Anthopoulos remembers. Once they arrived, Beinfest, flanked by Hill and assistant GM Dan Jennings, and Anthopoulos, surrounded by LaCava, Tinnish, Sartori, and Minasian, got down to business. Beinfest said the Marlins had closely examined the Blue Jays farm system and that for Josh Johnson they'd need elite prospects like pitcher Justin Nicolino and shortstop Adeiny Hechavarria. Anthopoulos replied, "We'll talk about anybody if it's the right guys, but if you ask him [pointing to his left at Tinnish], I don't think he'll be too excited talking about [trading] any of our guys." Tinnish, the former scouting director who drafted many of the team's top prospects, looked sheepish until Jennings countered by saying, "Shoot, you guys got *Snydergaard* [he meant elite pitching prospect Noah *Syndergaard*] and all these guys." Anthopoulos repeated that everybody was on the table, but not for Johnson, a pitcher with only one year of contractual control. "We'd have to expand the deal," he said. The Marlins, the Blue Jays figured, didn't do things halfway, so if they were going to move Johnson, chances are they'd move a host of others.

Anthopoulos proceeded to ask about Buehrle, and after a discussion about the left-hander, he inquired once more about Bonifacio. Finally at the end, he asked again about Reyes, the dazzling shortstop he had long coveted. Beinfest was receptive, saying the Marlins had lost their way and needed to get back to what they did best, which was drafting and developing players. In about 40 minutes, a rough outline for a blockbuster with the potential to reshape the Blue Jays as a franchise had taken shape. But as the meeting was wrapping up, Anthopoulos told his counterparts, "I have no idea if I can take on that money. Maybe we'll talk about money coming back in the deal," The Marlins said they were open to anything in the right trade. Before the meeting ended, they told Anthopoulos, "We think you've got as good of minor-league talent as there is in the game, and you guys have a lot of fits." And with that, they parted ways.

As the Blue Jays contingent walked back to the main lobby at the Hyatt, Sartori turned to Anthopoulos and said, "I knew you were going to ask about Reyes. You couldn't help yourself, huh?" Anthopoulos smiled, but already his mind was elsewhere. It was about 6:45 p.m. back in Toronto, and team president Paul Beeston was still in the office. Anthopoulos remembers passing by Dodgers GM Ned Colletti and his wife on the path before ducking under a palm tree to phone Beeston.

"I've got a chance to get Johnson, Buehrle, and Reyes," he said.

"Which one?" answered Beeston.

"All of them," Anthopoulos replied.

Beeston was skeptical.

"At first I told him there was no way he'd do the deal with Florida, not because we wouldn't do it but because they wouldn't do it," Beeston recalls. "You might get one of them, but this is a bait and switch, trust me. If you've ever seen a bait and switch, this is it. They're coming with those guys and they're going to give you three guys that they don't want and maybe one of the guys, most likely Johnson because he's the free agent at the end of the year, and that's all you're getting. They're talking [Jake] Marisnick, they're talking Hechavarria, they're talking all these guys we have rated high, Syndergaard, [Aaron] Sanchez. There's no way they're doing this deal, not a chance."

Still, Beeston called Rogers Communications CEO Nadir Mohamed that night and told him what was happening, and asked for a special payroll allowance again. The money would impact the 2013 budget almost the same as the thwarted Peavy deal, but had significant implications for 2014 and beyond. Mohamed agreed to look at it, and a conference call with Anthopoulos was scheduled for Saturday morning.

BACK IN CALIFORNIA, DELEGATES for all 30 teams were invited to a party at one of the palatial homes belonging to the Lerner family, who own the Washington Nationals. The Blue Jays group spread out that night, chatting up different contacts, taking pains to avoid the Marlins so as to not tip their hand. "It was like we didn't even know each other," said Anthopoulos.

Once the party ended, they returned to their suite, pulled up the files on all the players they had discussed with the Marlins, plotted the salary implications on a payroll spreadsheet, and played out various scenarios until 2 a.m. At the end of the session, Anthopoulos turned to his staff and said, "Assuming we can do this financially, this is the deal we're going to spend all our time on. Forget everything else."

On their way to the airport the next afternoon, Anthopoulos called Beinfest and told him that he wanted to make the deal but needed a day or two to clear the contracts with ownership. Beinfest understood. The next morning, Saturday, November 10, Anthopoulos was in the office along with Beeston for a conference call with Mohamed, who dissected the deal in a 15-minute conversation and offered his approval on the finances, provided they felt the trade made sense from a baseball perspective.

"It's not one of those ones that was a tough sell," says Beeston. "Nadir gets full credit for this, nobody else, because he could have said yes or no, but that relationship was built over a long period of time. He bought into it."

Adds Anthopoulos, "Nadir is amazing. He has this innate ability to ask the right questions right away. Within five minutes, he can know every which way things can develop and he's prepared for them."

A caveat Anthopoulos added was that the deal might not happen if the Marlins' price was too high. Internal discussion about which prospects the Blue Jays would be willing to surrender started almost immediately.

Once the Blue Jays had their house in order, Anthopoulos engaged Beinfest in an intense series of offers and counteroffers, sometimes coming as quickly as 30 minutes apart. One would call the other and open with, "Do you have a pen?"

A holdup was that Anthopoulos kept asking for Bonifacio, and the Marlins wouldn't include him in their counters, while Beinfest wanted Jeff Mathis, whom the Blue Jays refused to give up. But the form of a deal came together over the weekend. By Monday night, when Anthopoulos headed to the Loblaws up the road from his house to do some grocery shopping, he was looking at Johnson, Buehrle, Reyes, and Bonifacio heading to Toronto, and Henderson Alvarez, Yunel Escobar, Anthony DeSclafani, Hechavarria, Nicolino, and Marisnick to Miami. "I only get to go shopping late at night when I'm coming home from work," says Anthopoulos. "We had the baby, and I was still going out to buy stuff." On his way back to the house, he called Beinfest again, and ended up driving around the block several times to finish the conversation before pulling into his driveway. They agreed to talk again the next morning. "My wife was like, 'How come you were at the grocery store so long?'"

On Tuesday morning, the Marlins called, insisting the Blue Jays add Mathis and take John Buck in return. They were including $8.5 million in cash and wanted the Blue Jays to take on the $6 million due to Buck. Anthopoulos refused, and the deal was off. "We'd just signed Jeff Mathis, and I just didn't feel like Jeff needed to be in this deal," he explains.

The GM and his inner circle were in a sombre mood as they went to lunch. "They were like, 'If Paul knew this he'd kill you,'" Anthopoulos recalls. "'You're really not going to do this deal because of Jeff Mathis–John Buck?'" They were right. Beeston says he would have hit the roof had he known.

"You can't kill the deal for Buck. You're going to kill the deal for John Buck?" Beeston continues. "You mean to tell me we're going to get back two pitchers, Reyes, one of my favourite players, and Bonifacio. We're going to have a track team. We're selling entertainment, that's what it's all about."

Eventually, Anthopoulos relented, called Beinfest back and agreed to the deal, and then phoned Beeston, who was anxiously awaiting updates while attending a Loblaws board meeting. There were physicals for 12 players to be arranged and because of the amount of money changing hands, commissioner Bud Selig would have to approve the trade.

Word of the pending transaction leaked around dinnertime Tuesday, and a buzz about the Blue Jays electrified baseball fans across the country, washing away the lingering distaste from 2012's misery and Farrell's departure. "I think we kind of told baseball that we're going to be a factor next year," closer Casey Janssen, the club's most tenured player, said that night. Indeed, perception around the industry changed in a heartbeat.

"The Blue Jays went from a four to an eight and a half in one day," said Johnson's agent, Matt Sosnick, who was shocked that the Blue Jays pulled off such a big deal. "I look at this as a poker game, and Alex as the guy who's folded 50 hands in a row, everyone's forgotten he's at the table, and then he goes all in on a pair of aces."

The only person not revelling in the moment was the man who helped orchestrate it.

"As crazy as it is, I was bummed out that day," Anthopoulos says. "I can remember calling everybody else, Henderson, Yunel, [and] the development guys called the kids, but calling Jeff, saying, 'I just signed you and now I'm trading you,' that was not fun to do. I really struggled with it. He was shocked, he said, 'Look, I wanted to be here, especially with all these changes you're about to make; I didn't sign here to leave.' He was so polite, so professional, but said, 'Hey, I'm not happy. I don't want to go.'

"To this day it still bothers me that I did it. Because it was so fresh it felt like a betrayal [of Mathis]. It's terrible to say but it's true. It just didn't feel right, but at the same time it's a $160 million transaction that could transform the organization. That's understandable, too. Paul was like, 'What's wrong with you? It's business.' Call me soft or weak or whatever, it bothered me."

The malaise, however, did not last long.

IMMEDIATELY, ANTHOPOULOS OPENED A new front of activity when he engaged in talks with free agent Melky Cabrera. The Blue Jays envisioned him playing left field and batting second between Reyes and Jose Bautista, and used that in their pitch to his agents, Seth and Sam Levinson.

Left field had turned into a black hole for the Blue Jays. With Travis Snider and Eric Thames both dealt for relief pitching the previous July, their only in-house candidates were talented but raw rookies Anthony Gose and Moises Sierra.

Cabrera was far more proven, but what kind of player he'd be clean, after a positive test for elevated levels of testosterone spoiled his breakout season, was no certainty. Anthopoulos recognized the potential buy-low opportunity immediately after Cabrera's 50-game suspension was handed down, prompting the Blue Jays to do background work on him.

The reports on his time with the Kansas City Royals and Giants were good, Bautista and Edwin Encarnacion both liked him a lot, and by Friday, November 16, the Blue Jays settled on a $16 million, two-year deal with Cabrera. Because of the drug suspension, it was a risk, but one Anthopoulos was willing to take. He didn't want to count on kids, was wary of a weak free agent market in 2014, and wasn't prepared to make an expensive commitment to other free agents like Michael Bourn or Nick Swisher. "We felt like he was going to give us plus defence in left, play all three outfield spots, which is valuable if someone gets hurt. He can run, make some contact, and switch hit," says Anthopoulos.

Over the weekend Reyes, back from an abbreviated Dubai vacation, became the last of the 12 players in the deal to take his physical. Meanwhile, Selig worked through the approval process — a touchy one for him given Miami's outrage over another sell-off despite a new taxpayer-funded stadium.

On Monday, November 19, the commissioner's office made the deal official with a statement from Selig that read: "It is my conclusion that this transaction, involving established major-leaguers and highly regarded young players and prospects, represents the exercise of plausible baseball judgement on the part of both clubs, does not violate any express rule of Major League Baseball, and does not otherwise warrant the exercise of any of my powers to prevent its completion. It is, of course, up to the clubs involved to make the case to their respective fans that this transaction makes sense and enhances the competitive position of each, now or in the future."

Cabrera's signing was also made official that day, but Anthopoulos didn't speak with the media until the next morning, when he took the podium to discuss two of the most remarkable off-season weeks Blue Jays fans have ever seen.

All the points of priority — two starters, an infielder, a reliever, and a left fielder — were addressed in one fell swoop. But the Blue Jays still had more up their sleeve.

THE NEW OLD MANAGER | 2

JOHN GIBBONS JOKES THAT he was seldom recognized on the street during his first term as manager. And during a Toronto visit in November 2012, he preferred to keep it that way. After consummating a jaw-dropping trade with the Miami Marlins, the Blue Jays were still without a manager, and while no one, including Gibbons, expected him to be a candidate, he would surely arouse suspicion if spotted.

On the evening of November 17, Gibbons was to meet assistant general manager Tony LaCava and pro scouting director Perry Minasian for dinner at Morton's, an upscale steakhouse on Avenue Road. "I'm standing out front, waiting on them, and one of the guys says, 'You look familiar. Did you used to coach here?' I said yeah. He says, 'What are you doing here?' I said, 'I came up here for a wedding.'"

At that moment, he did not know how fitting his metaphor was. Alex Anthopoulos had called him earlier in the week and invited him to visit, talk about old times, maybe discuss job opportunities. Both Anthopoulos and Gibbons thought at the time that a coaching job might work, but the GM was not about to force a coach on the new manager, whoever that turned out to be. Anthopoulos insists that his original weekend agenda did not include offering Gibbons the skipper's job.

After John Farrell's inelegant departure for Boston — "If memory serves me correct, I was traded," he would say later — Anthopoulos was in no hurry to hire a replacement. His first priority was roster renovation, beginning with the starting rotation. While the Miami trade awaited commissioner Bud Selig's rubber stamp, Anthopoulos finally began to think about his next manager.

Before hiring Farrell, who had never managed at any level, Anthopoulos had undertaken an exhaustive search. It was his first time through the process and he had compiled a long list of qualities he sought in a manager. "You're looking to try to get every box checked. There's no question it was much more academic," he says of the process. "Obviously, how do you know what the end game is going to be unless [a manager has] done it before?"

Neither Anthopoulos nor Farrell had done it before, and it ended badly. But this time would be different, the GM vowed. Having interviewed close to 20 candidates before settling on Farrell, and having seen that hire go sour, Anthopoulos was determined to rely on his instincts rather than a checklist. He also made a point of consulting two rival general managers whose opinions he respected. "Both were like, 'Dude, there's no way I'd hire someone I didn't know,'" he said.

Still, Gibbons was not in the picture. It was a bizarre notion, bringing back a former manager, especially one with a .500 record, and especially so soon. Anthopoulos interviewed at least three candidates — Jays coaches Brian Butterfield and Luis Rivera, and Los Angeles Dodgers' third-base coach Tim Wallach — but hadn't made up his mind when, for reasons he says he can't fully explain, he decided to invite Gibbons to town for a chat.

"Once I got to talking with him, it was like — 'right in front of your eyes,'" Anthopoulos says. Their conversation took him back to Gibbons's first term, when then-GM J.P. Ricciardi and assistants Anthopoulos and Bart Given would descend on the manager's office after each home game and review what happened. Those sessions were easy and cordial. Some managers prefer that the GM stay out of the clubhouse, but Gibbons never felt threatened. Often, he and Anthopoulos had long discussions on their own.

"If you have a good relationship with a guy, there's a lot of give and take," Gibbons says. "You can have your battles and there's nothing personal. If there's some tension or a little animosity there, I think that could be tough, especially after tough losses. But when you have good relationships, you get a lot of benefit out of rehashing things and bouncing things off each other. I valued that. I was amongst friends there."

He and Anthopoulos rekindled that mood in November 2012. On the night of Sunday, November 18, Anthopoulos asked Gibbons what he thought about returning as manager. "I said, 'I'd love to, but you got no chance with that. No way you can pull that off.' Alex said, 'You never know.'"

Anthopoulos told him not to leave town. He would call the next day.

ON MONDAY, NOVEMBER 19, Anthopoulos walked into Paul Beeston's office and committed heresy: he closed the door. The president and general manager's offices are side by side, and Beeston never closes his door. He and Anthopoulos often converse through the open doors. "Alex, get in here." "Paul, you gotta see this." It can get loud, jocular, and profane. They have that kind of relationship.

On this day, Anthopoulos felt the discussion required a closed door. "This is serious," Anthopoulos said. "Before you interject here, just hear me out. This is really important to me. This isn't a joke."

Anthopoulos summarized his reasons: Gibbons handled the bullpen better than any other Toronto manager; he was a good evaluator of talent; and he got along well with his players, earned their respect, and demanded accountability. But the point Anthopoulos kept stressing was simply that he and Gibbons knew and liked each other, and would have a comfortable working relationship.

When Anthopoulos finished, Beeston said, "Are you shitting me?"

At first, Beeston admitted, the idea of Gibbons coming back was a "shock." But it didn't take long for him to agree with everything Anthopoulos said.

"Those are the points that he made, that there was a relationship there and he knew [they] could have a relationship," says Beeston. "The relationship with John [Farrell] would have been an acquired relationship because they were different personalities, and more importantly than that, he really didn't know John. He knew Gibby, he knew he could work with him, he knew Gibby's strengths, he knew Gibby's weaknesses, and he admired his ability to run the bullpen — the bullpen being a big problem. All that weighed on me, but the last part of it was, if [Anthopoulos] is going to be successful, he's going to have to have his manager . . . I can't force someone on him, and he seriously wanted [Gibbons], and I think at the end, he was right."

Anthopoulos had considered that the fans and media would consider the move absurd. He warned Beeston, "We could get hammered over this." Beeston said they'd been hammered throughout 2012. "What's one more?"

The next day, in a news conference called to discuss the Miami trade, Anthopoulos walked in with Gibbons in tow. He declared Gibbons "perfect" for the job. Perhaps because the trade had generated such widespread euphoria, or because the fan base benignly accepted the GM's logic, the Jays did not get hammered over the Gibbons hiring. Not then, anyway. Gibby was back, he had a great team to run, and all was right in the Blue Jays' world. Given the hoopla surrounding the redecorated roster, the choice of manager was almost background noise.

As he waded through his first three years on the job, Anthopoulos gradually learned that when the chips were down, he should follow his instincts. The decisions he made that ignored his instincts, he says, "are the ones that burned me." He refuses to say whether he ignored his instincts when he hired Farrell. But before he closed Beeston's door, he says he knew he was right about Gibbons.

"This guy's the best guy," Anthopoulos says. "He's right for this club, he's right for me, right for the organization. I don't care if he's been here 100 times. He's the right guy."

During the news conference introducing Gibbons as his new manager, Anthopoulos added this coda: "I've got more conviction in this transaction, in this hiring, than I've had in any," he said. "I can sleep like a baby at night because I know this was the right decision."

TWO MONTHS LATER, as he was preparing to leave for spring training, Gibbons sat at the dining-room table in his San Antonio home and discussed the sudden shift in his life path. During the previous season, when he managed the minor-league San Antonio Missions, he had spent more time at home than he had in years. Until Anthopoulos called, he had expected to return as manager of the local Double-A team, enjoying time with his wife, Julie, and three kids, when the Missions played at home. His mother, Sallie, and brother, Bill, live nearby, too. (His father, who retired as a colonel after 30 years in the air force, died in 2007. His sister, Kirstin, lives in Reno, Nevada.)

"I thought it was wonderful when he was here with the Missions for those young players to be around him," says Sallie Gibbons. "He's a really good role model. I thought that was the perfect job."

Her son had thought so, too. But to a baseball lifer, nothing beats the big leagues, especially if it means being back among friends. The Toronto offer was that much better because he hadn't craved it, hadn't expected it. Now, suddenly, he had rejoined the exclusive, 30-man club of big-league managers, inherited an elite roster, and stepped into a spotlight of soaring expectations.

In late January, before the day-to-day realities took over, before the relentless media attention began to wear on him, before the mounting injuries sabotaged his team, before the bewildering early-season losses began to mount, John Gibbons was relaxed and confident as he discussed the high hopes for his team.

"I think the biggest challenge is to get them all to pull together as a team and focus on one goal: to win this thing," he says. "I think this is a good group. I don't think there'll be any problem with that, but we have a lot of new faces in different spots, different experience levels. With so much change in such a short time, it just doesn't gel overnight."

Gibbons hadn't changed since his first term as Blue Jays manager. He would remain calm and upbeat through whatever storms arose. He yearned to manage a winner, but as always, he would also savour baseball beyond the wins and losses, the special camaraderie of a baseball family, the part that lasts. This was going to be fun, he said. "Maybe it's because in this business you never have to grow up," he says with a smile. "You can be a kid. Maybe it takes you back to your youth, I don't know. I mean, you do have to grow up *a little bit*." He laughed. "In a lot of ways, I'm embarrassed to say that. We're not solving the world's problems. We're in the entertainment business, playing a kid's game. We're supplying a little entertainment to make people feel better. That ain't a bad thing either."

FROM GOOSE BAY TO THE BLUE JAYS

3

ON A SUNNY FRIDAY afternoon in June 2008, Alex Anthopoulos took a long walk down the right-field line in PNC Park in Pittsburgh, hopped from the warning track into the stands, and took a seat in the empty stadium. He was an emotional wreck. "It was one of the worst days of my life," he recalls.

Two years into his term as assistant general manager, Anthopoulos had turned 31 a month earlier. He was experiencing a lot of firsts in the job, and he had just experienced another one. With his boss doing the heavy lifting, Anthopoulos sat in a Pittsburgh hotel room and watched J.P. Ricciardi fire John Gibbons, a friend to both of them.

For Anthopoulos, the moment remains vivid. "Gibby said, 'I'm sorry I let you guys down.' I even get choked up when I think back to the day. He's just such a great person. He was a good manager." He pauses. "It was just, 'We have to do *something*.'"

After raising hopes and teasing expectations with a 20-10 May, the Jays had gone 4-14 in June. They limped into Pittsburgh after absorbing three embarrassing losses in Milwaukee. In three weeks, they had fallen from three games out of first place to 10 and a half games behind.

Ricciardi decided that Gibbons, his former minor-league roommate, had to go.

With the deed done and Cito Gaston disinterred as manager, Anthopoulos came to the park, walked down the line, and called Gibbons. His eyes grow moist as he remembers.

"I was just a mess," he says. "I just wanted to say, 'Hey, thanks for everything.'"

JOHN GIBBONS WALKS AND talks Texas, but his baseball roots are in Canada. He first played on a ramshackle diamond not far from their family home on the second floor of a duplex in Happy Valley–Goose Bay, Labrador. But baseball did not begin well for John Gibbons. He was eight years old, and his stomach was churning as his dad drove him to his first Little League tryout on the grounds of Goose Bay Air Force Base. When they arrived, the kid who would become a number one draft pick could not move. He was terrified.

"My father said, 'Well, all right, you're not gonna play, son, if you don't get out of the car.' So I missed the tryouts," he recalls. "I was scared to death. I didn't know what this game was about. Luckily, a guy he worked with in his office on the base was coaching one of the teams and they needed a player. I started out as a right fielder, out there picking daisies."

The Gibbons family lived on the base grounds, where his father, Major William Gibbons, was a member of a United States Air Force contingent. Bill and Sallie Gibbons had met in their native Boston, and by the time Bill's military career took him to Goose Bay, they had a daughter and two sons in tow. John was the youngest.

Over the long winter, when the snow drifted above the first-floor windows of the Gibbons residence, huge snowplows cleared tunnel-like paths from the homes on the street. During the brief summer, black flies pestered a populace pursuing warm-weather pleasures. Baseball was one of those pleasures for John's older brother, Bill, who had learned the game when the family was stationed in Puerto Rico. Eventually, it would become John's passion.

John Gibbons was born in Great Falls, Montana, the first military assignment for his father, an air force optometrist whose later training led him to conduct pioneering research into night-vision technology for the military. Goose Bay was the fourth stop in Bill Gibbons's air force career that eventually took the family to San Antonio, Texas, where they stayed for John's teen years and eventually settled. While his parents retained their distinctive Massachusetts accents, John's drawl is conspicuously old west. "He is all Texan," his mother says.

His parents were athletic. Bill was captain of his high school football team. Sallie played field hockey and basketball, and became an avid equestrian. Her father was a semi-pro catcher in Massachusetts. John is named after him.

JOHN ALSO BECAME A catcher, in the way many young players do: his team needed one. He was on a Little League team in Houston, where his dad was taking advanced courses, when he put on the cumbersome equipment and squatted behind the plate. "I got too close to the batter," he remembers. "The first swing, the guy hit me right on the back of the head." He was undeterred, and soon he came to enjoy the action. It was better than picking daisies in right field. "If you're catching, at least you're doing something," he says.

By grade 11, it was clear that John Gibbons was doing something special on the baseball field. His expectations rose. He was invited to a Cincinnati Reds tryout camp at San Jacinto College in Houston. "That kind of lit the fire," he says. "Somebody's looking at you. Everybody wants to play pro ball and I thought, 'Here's my chance.' It was just a tryout camp so you weren't getting the best competition, but I thought, 'I can do this.' I dedicated myself to improving and building my strength up. I had a real good year my senior year."

Gibbons impressed scouts from major-league teams and prominent college programs. The University of Texas offered a scholarship. And the Blue Jays were among the big-league clubs that went to San Antonio to give him a private tryout. He heard rumours that they might make him their first-round pick in the 1980 amateur draft, but they chose Garry Harris, a high school shortstop from San Diego. Harris was the second overall pick in the draft, right behind Darryl Strawberry, but he never made it past Double-A.

The New York Mets had three picks in the first round. They took

Strawberry, then Billy Beane at number 23 overall, and Gibbons at number 24. Strawberry became a demon-plagued star; Beane flamed out as a player but rose to fame as a general manager; and Gibbons spent 11 seasons catching in the minors. The Mets promoted him to the majors twice and let him play in 18 games. He batted .220 with one home run.

EVEN THOUGH HIS BIG-LEAGUE playing career consisted of two cups of coffee, Gibbons did enjoy a taste of the World Series, albeit in a most unusual way — by sharing a bullpen with a squadron of police on horseback.

It was 1986, and after Gibbons played eight games during a late-season call-up, the Mets kept him around as a bullpen catcher for the playoffs. In the memorable Game 6 of the World Series, with the Mets trailing the Red Sox three games to two, Gibbons could not even see the field when one of baseball's historic events unfolded. The horses were blocking his view.

The Mets had scored twice in the bottom of the 10th inning to tie the score at 5-5 before Mookie Wilson hit the ground ball that famously eluded Boston first baseman Bill Buckner, capping an improbable Mets win in Shea Stadium.

"I was down there in the pen and [Dwight] Gooden was getting loose in case we just tied it," Gibbons recalls. "There in Shea, they had all the mounted police ready to storm the field if Boston won it. All the horses are lined up inside the bullpen against the outfield fence. I'm catching Gooden and his fastball is cracking the mitt pretty good, so every time the ball hit the mitt those horses were jumping. That's what I remember most. I didn't actually see it all happen because I was blocked by the horses."

Gibbons and the horses were stationed in the bullpen again the following night, when the Mets won it all. He did not join the mob scene on the field, but headed straight to the clubhouse where all of the Mets, stars and bit players alike, whooped it up in a champagne-soaked celebration.

It was his only taste of World Series bubbly. Twenty-seven years later, as he surveyed the roster he would manage in his second tour with the Blue Jays, he began to dream of tasting it again.

JOHN GIBBONS AND J.P. RICCIARDI met in 1981 when both played for the low Class A Shelby Mets in North Carolina. Ricciardi was a fast-talking infielder from Massachusetts, Gibbons a drawling catcher out of Texas, but they hit it off and wound up sharing a house with another player and the team's public relations director.

"We had one bed," Gibbons recalls. "So we'd rotate bed, couch, floor, floor. Didn't have a care in the world. J.P. was in that rotation. That's where we became good friends."

That was the second and final year in Ricciardi's playing career. Gibbons would play on for nine more seasons, becoming a decent Triple-A catcher and earning a roster spot with the Mets in spring training of 1984. But just before the exhibition season ended, he took an elbow to the face from Joe Lefebvre of the Phillies — "a cheap shot," Gibbons says — in a collision at home plate. After recovering from a cracked cheekbone, he went 1-for-25, hurt his elbow making a throw, missed two months, and wound up back in the minors. The following winter, his expectations declined further when the Mets resolved their catching situation by acquiring Gary Carter from the Montreal Expos.

"I wasn't bad compared to other catchers around the league, but they expected more," Gibbons says. "If I'd played better, I might've gotten another shot."

At 29, he knew he was destined to stay in Triple-A. So when the Mets offered him a job as a minor-league catching instructor, he accepted, launching a career as a minor-league coach and manager that lasted 12 years. Early on, he crossed paths again with Ricciardi, who was scouting for the Mets. "It was just like old times," Gibbons says of their chat during a flight from Boston to visit the Mets Triple-A team in Norfolk, Virginia. Ultimately, that relationship proved a boon when, in spring 2002, Gibbons needed a job. The new general manager of the Blue Jays asked if he was willing to be the bullpen catcher. It was not what Gibbons had in mind, but he needed a paycheque.

"I go to spring training, first day, hadn't squatted in 10 years, I go down there to the bullpen and squat down and my knee exploded on me, swelled up. I get the MRI, they say you got no cartilage. You can't catch during spring training."

The knee continued to bother him after the season began, and he thought he might have to quit. But then in June, Ricciardi fired manager Buck Martinez, promoted Carlos Tosca, shook up the coaching staff, and made Gibbons the first-base coach. "That saved me, physically and mentally and financially," he says.

A little more than two years later, Ricciardi fired Tosca. The GM's surprise choice for manager was his former minor-league roommate, the easygoing coach with a John Wayne gait and a ready smile. In two and a half years, John Gibbons had risen from bullpen catcher to manager, moving up as others moved out.

He stayed in the job for almost four years, the longest-serving skipper of the Ricciardi regime. It was a tumultuous time. The GM, mandated to chop payroll when he took over, had vowed to build a winner through shrewd drafting and player development. Then, owner Rogers Communications changed course. Given a hefty increase in payroll, Ricciardi began to sign prominent free agents to long-term contracts. It didn't work. When Gibbons was fired, he had a .500 record, appropriately symbolic of the teams he had led.

Along the way, Gibbons had developed a close relationship with Anthopoulos, whom Ricciardi originally hired as a 26-year-old scouting coordinator. In baseball, jobs most often flow from relationships, and among the many friends Gibbons had made along the way, Ricciardi and Anthopoulos proved pivotal.

"I knew the right guy, I knew the GM," he says of his first term as manager. "I still know the right guy. But I didn't think there'd be a second go-round."

Blue Jays fans could not quite believe it either. When they heard the news that Gibbons was coming back, two other names came immediately to mind: Shea Hillenbrand and Ted Lilly.

ANOTHER SIDE OF JOHN GIBBONS

4

WHATEVER ELSE HAPPENED DURING his first term as manager, John Gibbons is remembered most for two incidents that were remarkably out of character: his clubhouse confrontation with Shea Hillenbrand during a team meeting, and his tussle with Ted Lilly behind the dugout during a game. Those clashes took place about a month apart in summer 2006, which also happened to be Gibbons's most successful season as manager.

Over nearly two years as their skipper, players had never heard Gibbons raise his voice. "Even if we were playing bad he didn't really come in and yell," says Frank Catalanotto, who spent 14 years in the majors and joined the Jays in 2004, a few months before Gibbons took over. "I've had some managers, you lose five or six games in a row and they go bonkers. Gibby wasn't like that."

On Wednesday, July 19, no one had reason to believe he would be like that. Hillenbrand had been away from the team since the previous Saturday, joining his wife in California, where they completed their adoption of a baby girl. The Hillenbrands lived in Arizona, and the out-of-state paperwork was more complicated and time consuming than they expected. Hillenbrand arrived at the Rogers Centre shortly before game time Tuesday afternoon. Gibbons did not put him in the lineup.

27

The next night, Gibbons decided to keep Hillenbrand on the bench again, but not for disciplinary reasons, as Hillenbrand would claim.

"There was no discipline involved," Gibbons says. "He was away just like you'd be for a birth. I had no problem with it. That's big. That's your family."

As he filled out his lineup, the manager checked Hillenbrand's record against that night's starter, Kevin Millwood of the Texas Rangers. Hillenbrand was hitless in nine at-bats.

"He's been gone a few days," Gibbons says. "I figured the day he comes back he can go through BP, get readjusted for a day, be right back in there the next night. If he'd had great numbers against this guy, he'd have been in there. It was that simple."

But Hillenbrand, who had complained all season about his designated-hitter role — he wanted to play on defence as well — saw his benching as an affront. Baseball rules allow three days for parental leave and Hillenbrand had been late; general manager J.P. Ricciardi had refused even to look at him when he came on the field and now management was punishing him further, he said. No Blue Jays official had congratulated him on the adoption, he added. He blurted all that out in an angry, awkward, on-the-record discussion with several reporters during batting practice. He also said he expected to be traded.

Then, after batting practice, he went into the clubhouse and wrote "This ship is sinking" on a whiteboard. (The Jays' record was 52-40 and they had won five of their past six games.) Although some players found it amusing, "most of the guys thought it was bullshit and didn't like it," Catalanotto says. A coach saw it and told Gibbons. A few minutes later, teammate Gregg Zaun erased the message.

About an hour before game time, Gibbons called a team meeting and demanded to know who had written on the whiteboard. Hillenbrand acknowledged he had done it.

Gibbons exploded. "You think you're a man?" he shouted. "You're not a man. If you're a man, come on and fight me."

Around the room, jaws dropped. No one moved, including Hillenbrand. Like his teammates, he was dumbfounded. No one had ever seen this side of the affable skipper.

"Gibby was about a half an inch from his face the whole time," says Catalanotto, who estimated that the harangue lasted 10 minutes. Another player said it probably took about five minutes, but seemed longer. Hillenbrand seethed in silence.

Recalls Vernon Wells, "It was the most intense meeting I've ever been a part of."

"I've never seen anything like it in my life," Catalanotto says. "Gibby was irate. Trust me, we were all on the edge of our seats because we thought a fight might break out." The even-tempered manager had morphed into a raging bull. Hillenbrand was prone to mood swings, by turns amiable and hot blooded. In their imaginations, the players weren't sure who might land the first blow, or the last.

Gibbons raged on. "As long as I'm here, you'll never play again," he told Hillenbrand. "I was going out on a limb," he says now. "I didn't tell J.P. I said that."

Gibbons refuses to specify what he said to Hillenbrand. "It was not something my mother would be proud of," he adds. "I just unloaded. I got out some frustrations, I guess you could say."

After Gibbons stormed out, Hillenbrand stood, his eyes moist, and delivered a short apology. According to a player who asked to remain anonymous, Hillenbrand said, "'Guys, I didn't mean for this to happen. I'm sorry.'"

Hillenbrand left the locker room. There was dead silence. Wells followed his shaken teammate into another room and tried to find the words to comfort him. As Wells perceived it, Hillenbrand's sarcastic joke, scrawled thoughtlessly on a whiteboard, had sparked a team crisis.

"A lot of what Shea said and did was meant in jest, but not everyone took it that way," Wells says. "I took him with a grain of salt, laughed, and moved on, but for some, it can rub you the wrong way."

Although his apology sounded sincere, Hillenbrand was fuming. Less than half an hour before the game began, he changed into a T-shirt and shorts, packed a suitcase, and angrily dragged it down the stairs from the clubhouse level to the underground parking lot. Shortly thereafter, likely after calling his agent, he returned to the clubhouse and put on his uniform. Sometime during that period, he was also in touch with Geoff Baker, a *Toronto Star* beat writer, who broke the news of the clubhouse clash.

Gibbons was right; Hillenbrand would not play for him again. Before the game ended, the club announced that he had been placed on waivers, and three days later he was traded to the San Francisco Giants. At the time, he was among the Jays' leading hitters with a .301 batting average and .821 OPS. Ricciardi said the split resulted from "irreconcilable differences."

Never hesitant to speak his mind, Hillenbrand was a moody sort, often complaining about playing time and his DH role. He could be upbeat and empathetic with his teammates; several counted him as a friend. And sometimes, Hillenbrand was distant, sullen, and arrogant. While some players thought Gibbons went too far when he raged at Hillenbrand, most felt that the manager had struck a blow for team integrity.

"Shea basically gave up on the season, gave up on everyone, and wrote that on the board," Catalanotto says. "As the manager, you've got to control those situations."

The confrontation staggered the entire team. While some say they don't think the incident affected the team's performance, the Jays dropped 13 of their next 20 games. Somewhere, cynical observers suggested, Hillenbrand must have been smiling.

"The whole thing was weird because we saw a side of Gibby we hadn't seen before," says the player who asked to remain anonymous. "We saw a side of Shea we hadn't seen before, where it really hit him, something finally hit him, where it was like, 'Guys, I'm really sorry.' It put everybody in check a little bit. We were just stunned by everything that happened on both sides."

Wells played for Gibbons throughout the manager's first term and came to know him well. "All he expected was for us to be on time, play the game right, and don't disrespect the game in any way," Wells says. "If you ask Shea, he'd say he brought all that on himself."

THE HILLENBRAND FUROR HAD barely subsided when, a month later, Gibbons and Lilly nearly came to blows during an embarrassing loss to Oakland. Staked to an 8-0 lead after two innings, Lilly had given up five runs in the third and had two runners on base when Gibbons went to get the ball. Politely translated, Lilly said, "What are you doing here?" Gibbons barked back in kind. The brief, tense exchange filled TV screens across the country. Lilly finally gave up the ball. As he left the mound, he bumped Gibbons.

Instead of staying on the bench until the inning ended, as most deposed pitchers do, or going directly to the clubhouse, Lilly walked down the stairs into the tunnel just behind the dugout, where he began to pace back and forth. After handing the ball to reliever Jason Frasor, Gibbons spotted Lilly and made a beeline for the tunnel.

"Nothing premeditated," Gibbons says. "For some reason I just walked down there. I can't remember who said something first. We grabbed each other."

Immediately, players, trainers, and coaches rushed in and separated them. "I think the whole team was there," Gibbons says. He insists he did not emerge with a bloody nose, as some reports suggested. And in his office after the game, he and Lilly met again, this time in private. Each apologized.

"We were both shocked that it happened and embarrassed that it happened," Gibbons says.

Later that night, Catalanotto drove Lilly home. "Ted felt terrible about it," Catalanotto remembers. "He said, 'I screwed up, I shouldn't have done that.' He disrespected the manager."

SHEA HILLENBRAND'S BIG-LEAGUE CAREER ended at 31, a little over a year after his infamous confrontation with Gibbons. "He ran himself out of the game," Wells says. "He's talented enough that he can still hit at his level, but sometimes people don't get it until it's too late."

On the phone from his Arizona home, Hillenbrand is guarded when asked about the incident, but says it was one of several significant events that led to a profound change in his life. He found God, he says.

Regrets? "You can't live with regrets and you can't live with resentment," Hillenbrand says. "You forgive and you ask for forgiveness and that's how you learn. I utilized that incident in my life as a learning lesson. I was taught a lot from God about myself through that process, so I appreciate having that incident in my life. It was something that I needed."

Without saying so explicitly, he intimates that he was more upset with Ricciardi than with Gibbons on that day in 2006.

"A lot of my anger and a lot of my uneasiness had nothing to do with John Gibbons, and that's what people don't understand," he says. "John Gibbons is a really, really good person. He's a great family man. He's a really good players' manager. He's really easy to talk to and he's really easy to get along with. That's a huge plus for a ball team, especially for players like myself that knew how to play the game, that don't need to lean on or utilize anybody else."

Asked whether he was shocked at Gibbons's explosive response that day in the clubhouse, Hillenbrand pauses. His reply is vague. "That's a tough question to answer. I don't know that I can answer that." He will not elaborate, preferring to focus on his personal journey after baseball.

"I was at a point in my life where I wasn't saved," he says of his clash with his manager. "Now I'm saved. I have Jesus in my heart. It's an amazing accomplishment for myself to be able to experience that. So with the love in my heart now that I didn't have then, I'm a totally different person at this point. I don't harbour that anger in my heart any more."

IN THE DAYS THAT followed Gibbons's second coming as manager, the Hillenbrand and Lilly incidents were roundly rehashed in the media. They represented two of the 710 games Gibbons had managed, but they were so bizarre and so dramatic they remain indelible in his legacy.

"I managed almost four years there," Gibbons says, "and if you asked anybody what I was known for, if you took a poll, that would probably be the number one thing. That's not something I want. I'm a husband and father raising three kids. That's not who I am. I think I'm a very fair, understanding guy. I've got a lot of patience."

Most players agree. A man with a generally genial disposition had earned the respect of his troops and his superiors over 15 years as a minor- and major-league coach and manager. But after his first term as a big-league skipper, many remembered him as a hothead.

"I know Gibby wishes those things didn't happen," says infielder John McDonald, who had a front-row seat for both episodes. "I'm sure he wishes they didn't happen the way they did happen, but one way or another, he was going to take care of it. That's what I like about him. That's what players appreciate about him."

Steve Springer, a minor-league coach and scout for the Jays, is one of Gibbons's best friends. Springer got to know Gibbons in 1985 when they played together at Triple-A Norfolk. After living with Lenny Dykstra and Billy Beane that year, Springer was looking for a change of pace. He and Gibbons shared living quarters the next season.

"When you room with somebody for six months, you want somebody that's really low-maintenance, that's not going to fly off the handle at every little thing," Springer says. "He's just so even keel. It really makes me laugh how the media could blow it up that he's a hard-ass because of two incidents. If you don't get along with John Gibbons, trust me, you're the idiot."

5 | THE FINISHING PIECE

TO UNDERSTAND HOW RADICAL a departure the bold November moves were for the Toronto Blue Jays and Alex Anthopoulos, consider the following: Maicer Izturis's three-year deal was the first free-agent contract handed out by the GM to guarantee more than one season; and the Miami Marlins blockbuster pushed the club's payroll into nine figures for the first time at $120 million, up more than 20 percent from the previous high of $96 million in 2008.

Praise for the moves came from all corners. Fans, some of whom had become deeply disenchanted the previous winter when the Blue Jays failed to land Japanese starter Yu Darvish and never made a serious run at free-agent Prince Fielder, cheered the massive investment. Ticket sales soared. Media, both local and national, praised the Blue Jays' big step toward relevance. And Las Vegas oddsmakers quickly installed them as World Series favourites.

The transactions also restored an element of trust. To that point, repeated promises from Anthopoulos and team president Paul Beeston that the team would spend when the time was right had lost all meaning. But the fiscal responsibility the pair had shown in previous years paid dividends when they finally did ask Rogers Communications Inc. to ante up for arguably the riskiest single transaction in team history.

Beeston was convinced the right time had finally come. He describes his message to ownership this way: "If the deal makes sense and we think it's smart money then we'll come to you for the money. But I'm coming to you for the money, because I'm telling you right now, the risk is only in the amount of money you're committed, because if we pull this deal off we're going to generate more than that in revenue. If guys get hurt, if guys don't perform, then you're not going to make it to where you want, but if I take the salaries up $25 million, I expect to take the revenue up by more than $25 million. So where the fuck is the risk?"

Acknowledging the potential for injury and underperformance combined with the long-term contractual commitments, Beeston adds, "Off of what they've done, their track record, if they play and pitch to form, you've probably got a pretty good team. And so it wasn't one of those deals that I worried about."

Anthopoulos, though, still felt the Blue Jays were one elite arm away from being able to contend for an extended period. And like a good chess player, he was thinking several moves ahead while he wrapped up the Marlins blockbuster. John Buck, the catcher forced upon him by Miami counterpart Larry Beinfest, was one of the primary pieces in play.

"When I got traded, right away [Anthopoulos] told me he wasn't going to keep me and J.P. [Arencibia]," Buck recalls. "It was either going to be me or J.P., the best deal for the team, obviously."

But for what, or whom?

The Blue Jays had already explored other possibilities before making the Marlins deal. Aside from checking into Jake Peavy, Anibal Sanchez, and Hisashi Iwakuma, they had also asked the Oakland Athletics about Brett Anderson and the Chicago Cubs about Jeff Samardzija, and were turned away both times. The Tampa Bay Rays were preparing to move James Shields, but even after Anthopoulos told them Travis d'Arnaud, the elite catching prospect they had long coveted, was in play, along with any other prospect, talks didn't progress. The Rays had zeroed in on Kansas City Royals uber-prospect Wil Myers, and eventually, they landed him in a six-player deal.

The only arm likely still available in trade — the Blue Jays weren't seriously interested in free agents at that point — was reigning National League Cy Young Award winner R.A. Dickey, whose contract was due to expire after the 2013 season.

Anthopoulos first checked in on the knuckleballer at the GM meetings in California, on the same day as the fateful discussion with the Marlins. After the party at the Lerner mansion, a minibus shuttle service ferried guests back to the Hyatt Regency Indian Wells Resort & Spa, where everybody was staying.

While waiting at the shuttle depot, Anthopoulos ran into Mets GM Sandy Alderson, and sauntered over and said, "Hey Sandy, I just wanted to talk about R.A." When a shuttle arrived, they jumped in and settled into two different rows before Alderson, seated by a window, patted the spot beside him.

"Sit over here beside me so we can speak privately."

Anthopoulos moved over and sat to Alderson's right. Alderson said the Mets were trying to sign Dickey to a new deal.

"We probably won't know until after Thanksgiving, around that time," Alderson said. "We'll see where that goes."

"What do you think the chances are that you're going to sign him? Pretty good?"

"I don't know."

Anthopoulos figured he was at a dead end. "The fact he didn't say 'Yeah, we're open,' [means] I'm not going to bother [pursuing it]. 'We might' means you'll spend two months trying to get him. And then we just talked about all kinds of stuff."

He asked Alderson about his needs, and was told the Mets were looking for catching and outfield help, two areas of depth for the Blue Jays. Back at the hotel they parted ways. Anthopoulos reconnected with his crew and began work on the Marlins deal.

Dickey sat on the Blue Jays' back burner until November 21, the day after the mother of all news conferences in Toronto unveiled the Miami trade, Melky Cabrera's signing, and the return of John Gibbons as manager.

U.S. Thanksgiving was November 22. Thinking back to Alderson's timeline, Anthopoulos gave him a call. "Look, sorry I haven't gotten back to you," Alderson said. "I still need a little bit more time to work through some things. I'm not sure how this is developing. We're still trying to re-sign him."

But suddenly, extension talks between the Mets and Dickey (focusing on a three-year deal in the $22–$30 million range) took a turn for the worse. The following week, Alderson and Anthopoulos got hot and heavy in trade talks. The asking price started at d'Arnaud and pitcher Noah Syndergaard, two of the Blue Jays' most prized prospects. Sticker shock stalled the initial talks.

But the Mets had crossed a line in the sand, and Dickey knew it. When the Winter Meetings opened in his hometown of Nashville on December 3, "I felt like I was going to be traded just because of the way negotiations were going with the Mets, coupled with having a little bit of business sense, and knowing they were going to try to maximize their value in me," he says.

Dickey figured the Blue Jays were among the teams inquiring about him, as well as the Texas Rangers — the club that drafted him and launched his renaissance as a knuckleballer — the Baltimore Orioles, and the Los Angeles Angels.

But the four days at baseball's annual swap meet didn't move him any closer to a new home. Anthopoulos and Alderson held a single meeting that went nowhere. A week earlier they had been trading concrete proposals. All of a sudden they were talking concepts.

Then, during the following weekend, the James Shields shoe dropped. The Royals sent Myers, plus well-regarded young pitchers Jake Odorizzi and Mike Montgomery, and third baseman Patrick Leonard to the Rays for Shields and Wade Davis, leaving the Blue Jays at Dickey or bust.

Anthopoulos phoned Alderson and said, "Look, what's the bottom line on this thing? What is a done deal if I say, 'Yes, we can get this thing done'?"

"Syndergaard, d'Arnaud, and the [Wuilmer] Becerra kid," answered Alderson.

"If I come back to you, and I say yes, we have a deal?"

Alderson said yes.

Anthopoulos stressed that any deal would have to include the Mets taking John Buck to make the money work, and include Josh Thole as protection for the Blue Jays in case J.P. Arencibia got hurt. He also wanted a window to negotiate an extension with Dickey. The Mets agreed.

A more pivotal hurdle came December 12, when Anthopoulos and Beeston made another trip to the Rogers corporate offices to meet with CEO Nadir Mohamed, CFO Tony Staffieri, and Rogers Media head Keith Pelley to explain the payroll implications of the extension they planned to offer Dickey.

They got the approval that night. The next morning Anthopoulos called the Mets and set out his precise proposal: the Jays would get Dickey, Thole, and fellow catcher Mike Nickeas for d'Arnaud, Syndergaard, and Becerra (a lower-level prospect). The deal was contingent on the successful negotiation of a contract extension with Dickey.

The Mets agreed, granting the Blue Jays a 72-hour negotiating window, due to start the next morning. Anthopoulos asked his executive assistant, Anna Coppola, to find him the first available flight to Nashville. The negotiating window bothered the secretive Anthopoulos, who feared a leak would complicate the talks, and he was also unsure how talks would go with Dickey's agent, Bo McKinnis, whom he didn't know. Coppola found a flight at 4:30 p.m., booked seats for both her boss and pro scouting director Perry Minasian, who had been a clubhouse attendant with the Rangers when Dickey was there, and had a strong bond with the pitcher. Then she set up Gibbons on a flight from San Antonio to Nashville on Friday morning. They were sending in the troops and leaving nothing to chance.

With everything happening so quickly, Anthopoulos didn't have time to go home and pack. He grabbed his passport and the carry-on he keeps ready in the office for just such occasions. He collected the home and road No. 43 Blue Jays jerseys he asked travel director Mike Shaw to have made. And he tossed in a tax report for Dickey, which showed that the disparity between pitching in New York and Toronto on his $5 million salary was roughly $40,000. Minasian, who lives in Michigan and had just checked into the Renaissance Hotel attached to the Rogers Centre, ran down the hallway from the Blue Jays offices to the hotel lobby and up to his room, threw all his stuff in a bag, and scooted back to rejoin Anthopoulos.

"I literally sprinted like Carl Lewis, although I'm no Carl Lewis," he remembers with a chuckle.

During a stopover in Charlotte, Anthopoulos found a Brooks Brothers store at the airport and bought enough underwear, shirts, pants, and sweaters to last three days, then hustled over to make his connection, and picked up toiletries once they arrived in Nashville late Thursday night.

They were determined to descend on Dickey as soon as the window opened Friday morning, but the plan hit a snag when the Mets asked for a more detailed look at d'Arnaud's medical files. The catcher missed half the season with a torn posterior cruciate ligament in his left knee, and the talks between the Blue Jays and Dickey couldn't start until Alderson and his group became comfortable with the medical reports.

That didn't keep news about the pending trade from leaking; word that the Blue Jays were the leading contenders to land Dickey seeped out Friday night. Dickey followed the reports. His initial reaction? "Curious," he said. "I wasn't like, 'Oh God, Toronto, what the hell.' That was not it at all. It was much more, 'All right, Let's get on the internet and start looking at some things.' My wife and I sat in bed that night and started researching the city and tried to figure out if we did get traded where would we live, what could we take the kids to, to really expose them to things in a different country. We tried to immerse ourselves in what might be coming."

Meanwhile, Anthopoulos, Minasian, and Gibbons were sitting on their hands, waiting for the Mets to open the window, so on Friday night they decided to check out a movie. Minasian found a theatre right by their hotel. He also found positive reviews for *Sessions,* the only movie playing. The trio had no idea it was about a man confined to an iron lung who seeks to lose his virginity.

"That was an awkward movie to see with two other guys. It's more of a husband-wife type movie," Minasian says sheepishly. "We were trying to kill time. You go with reviews; it had good reviews, but I skipped the synopsis. It was good popcorn though. Those guys crushed popcorn; there were buckets everywhere, popcorn flying all over the place. So they can't complain about that." That didn't stop Anthopoulos and Gibbons from ripping on Minasian, already the subject of constant ribbing for waking up to attend 5 a.m. yoga classes at a nearby gym, for the choice of film. "They gave me a lot of shit for that. I got a lot of shit on that trip."

By Saturday morning, the Mets were ready to make the deal. The paperwork was submitted to Major League Baseball. Alderson phoned Dickey to tell him the news, then called Anthopoulos to open the window.

Within minutes Anthopoulos spoke with McKinnis and then was on the phone with Dickey, who was shocked that his new GM was already in town waiting for him. "It felt very intense at that point," he recalls, "like they're here, it's business time."

The Blue Jays trio initially met McKinnis for coffee at 4 p.m., and then McKinnis picked up Dickey en route to dinner. Both vehicles pulled into the parking lot at the same time. Minasian and Dickey spotted each other immediately. "Hey!" they yelled, before they ran over and hugged.

"You have no idea how bad I wanted to call you during all the rumours," Dickey told him.

"We wouldn't be here having this discussion if you just would have signed with us three years ago," Minasian quipped, in reference to his pursuit when Dickey was a minor-league free agent after the 2009 season. The Blue Jays had hoped to bring Dickey in as a depth arm that winter and Minasian says he called McKinnis "literally 100 times" before the pitcher signed with the Mets. Ultimately, Dickey felt there was more opportunity for him in New York and he had always wanted to pitch in the National League, having grown up in Nashville watching the Atlanta Braves and Chicago Cubs on TV.

Regardless, the Minasian-Dickey connection allowed everyone to speed through the entire feeling-out process, and get down to business in an atmosphere of trust. Anthopoulos presented Dickey with the two jerseys and the tax report, and then explained to him why the Blue Jays wanted him, how he fit in with the core he'd assembled, what the farm system had coming, and how he planned to sustain a winner. Gibbons described how he ran a team.

As Dickey absorbed the avalanche of information, he also wanted Anthopoulos and Gibbons to hear him out, to understand what they'd be getting and be certain they were comfortable with him as a person. "I talked to them about how much I enjoyed getting to pitch deeply in games and how much I enjoyed an open line of communication between the manager and myself, and how that allowed a modicum of success you might not have otherwise," remembers Dickey. "I got to enjoy that with Terry Collins in New York and felt that was very instrumental in the success I had. For instance, after the seventh inning, if he came over to me, we'd have a good talk about, 'Hey, what do you think, this is what I'm thinking about doing, how do you feel about doing that.' And I'd say, 'Yeah, I'm at my end, you should probably go ahead and make the move,' or 'No, I've got another inning.' I told them, 'I'm going to fight for this.' And they were okay with it."

By dinner's end, roughly around 9:30 p.m., everyone involved had come to understand Dickey was ready to do an extension. As McKinnis drove Dickey home, they discussed whether this was something the pitcher wanted to go through with, and whether he and his family would be comfortable moving north. "I wanted to be there, and came to that conclusion in the car with Bo on the way back," says Dickey. "I said, 'If we can work this out, I'm in.'"

The two men, both devout Christians, prayed together. Then McKinnis phoned Anthopoulos and asked him to meet at a pub to try to work out a contract. They stayed until it closed at 1 a.m., returned to the hotel where the Blue Jays contingent was staying, and talked in the lobby for another hour and a half. They made progress but decided to call it a night and reconnect on Sunday morning. Anthopoulos sent Minasian and Gibbons home on Sunday. Their work was done.

The GM spent the rest of the day going back and forth with McKinnis, trying to iron out how to value Dickey's 2016 club option and what the buyout should be. There was only so much wiggle room left. Ownership's approval was based on the contract value staying within a certain range, and the clock was ticking on both the negotiating window and the chance for Anthopoulos to make the last flight home to Toronto. "I was fried at that point," he says. "It was exhausting." A final push settled the deal: $29 million over three years, with a club option for $12 million in 2016 or a $1 million buyout. Anthopoulos scrambled to the airport and barely made his flight, arriving home around 11 p.m. Meanwhile, Dickey and his family began preparing for life with the Blue Jays.

"The way he went about the courtship," says Dickey, "I really appreciated it."

News of the trade continued to leak out in dribs and drabs over the weekend. It was officially announced the next day, December 17, and initially skeptical fans were suddenly caught up in Dickey-mania. His acquisition provided another spike in ticket sales and any concerns about moving d'Arnaud and Syndergaard — two elite prospects so much hope had been pinned on — gave way to euphoria over the addition of a Cy Young Award winner. That it came exactly three years and one day after the trade of Roy Halladay to the Philadelphia Phillies only underlined the franchise's sudden role reversal. "At first it was, 'We'd like to have him but we're not trading those guys,' but the more work you start doing on him . . ." Anthopoulos says, his voice trailing off. "How many opportunities do you have to get a front of the rotation starter?"

Not many, of course, and analysts on both sides of the border pointed to Dickey's acquisition as the finishing touch the team needed. The new staff depth meant that J.A. Happ, a mid-rotation starter at minimum for many big-league teams, entered spring training fighting for a job in the bullpen.

Vegas again increased the Blue Jays' odds of winning the World Series, and they appeared certain to end the post-season drought that dated back to 1993.

Yet the memory of past failures kept Anthopoulos sombre. "We're working our butt off to try and get better and we are, but it's painful when you're trading good young players you really like," he says one bright spring day. "After what we went through in 2012, how do you get excited about anything anymore?"

At that moment, he was unaware how prescient his words would become in the months ahead.

THE SPRING FORWARD | 6

DURING THE EARLY DAYS of spring training, reality rarely disturbs the reverie. Every year, players, coaches, and fans catch the fever. Spring training is about starting fresh, away from the grey, icy days of a northern winter, and luxuriating in sunshine and hope, even if the hope is patently false. "Don't try to act like baseball isn't romantic," Blue Jays pitching prospect Daniel Norris tweeted in January as spring-training daydreams danced in his head.

It has always been this way, even for the Toronto Blue Jays over the past two decades, when their championship ambitions were typically constructed of tissue paper, and sighs of "maybe next year" often began by Victoria Day. But the optimism of 2013 was built from stronger stuff. When pundits and fans alike predicted that the Blue Jays could go all the way, no one laughed.

So it was in February, when writers long jaded by the Jays' past failures entered the austere Dunedin clubhouse in Florida, and absorbed a refreshing set of sights and sounds. Just around the corner from the bulletin board by the door stood four lockers, whose occupants epitomized the hopes of 2013. Darren Oliver, the 42-year-old reliever, had returned from near retirement to reclaim the first locker and one last chance for a World Series ring. Next to him sat Mark Buehrle, another evergreen pitcher, who spent a prosperous decade with the Chicago White Sox and a turbulent year in Miami before joining the Jays in the stunning November trade. Adjacent to Buehrle sat Josh Johnson, also late of Miami, whose stuff, the critics said, might be the best on the staff. Johnson's immediate neighbour was R.A. Dickey, the 38-year-old pitcher who had become a near legend in his own time because, against all odds, he patched his tattered personal life and learned late in his career to make a knuckleball do things no one had ever seen.

The genial conversation on veterans' row was generally subdued. But a joyful cacophony arose from the far wall, where the bookend lockers were occupied by two Joses — Bautista and Reyes. From the outset, their noisy Spanish repartee, often shouted from one end of their long row to the other, set a buoyant tone. Between them stood 16 lockers, assigned mainly to Latino players, among them Maicer Izturis, Emilio Bonifacio, Henry Blanco, Melky Cabrera, and Edwin Encarnacion. Next to Blanco sat J.P. Arencibia, whose grandparents are from Cuba. They could compare notes on catching in two languages.

Brett Lawrie, the young, hyperkinetic Canadian-star-in-waiting, sat in the middle of the row, next to Mark DeRosa. A 15-year veteran, the articulate, intense, and fun-loving DeRosa was signed to serve as the Jays' 25th man, clubhouse oracle, and role model for Lawrie. To foster a good clubhouse atmosphere, "you've got to mesh the Latins and the Americans and the Canadians," says DeRosa, who played for seven big-league teams before joining Toronto. "At the end of the day, I have to feel that I can confide in them as much as they can confide in me."

When spring training opened, the Blue Jays appeared to be a team facing few significant roster questions. As a result of off-season trades and free-agent signings, the rotation was set, and the starting lineup virtually so. Izturis and Bonifacio would compete for the regular second-base assignment, Gibbons asserted in the early going; by the end of camp, he was saying they probably would share the job. One or two spots in the bullpen were available. The official spin said Blanco or Josh Thole would vie to back up starting catcher Arencibia, but all along, management had settled on the 41-year-old Blanco, who, like DeRosa, had a reputation as a solid clubhouse leader. "Pretty much we're the same, and do the same type of job," said Blanco. "We're going to be there for our teammates and our team." Adding to his appeal was that during their initial meeting, Dickey told general manager Alex Anthopoulos that Blanco could catch his knuckleball with "chopsticks."

In short, the Blue Jays looked like a team with no gaping holes. Its depth and the versatility of several capable players gave Gibbons uncommon flexibility, and a margin of error unheard of among Toronto clubs in this century. Gibbons knew first-hand about four of those clubs; he had managed them. His surprise hiring in December left him feeling lucky.

"To come back, I didn't expect that," Gibbons said, "and then to take over a team that's built this way, I'm just hoping it's meant to be — one of those things where everything's lined up just right."

So blessed, management set a tone of caution early on, warning all who would listen that talent alone could not assure a playoff spot. Players picked up the mantra in interviews. And late in spring training, when strength and conditioning coach Bryan King ordered his annual set of T-shirts for the players, he put this inscription on the back: *Nothing is given. Everything is earned.*

King started the T-shirt tradition when he took over the job in 2009. Previous tees promoted universal messages. *We will not be outworked. Appreciate the grind. Hard work is the foundation of success. One team, one goal.* "This year was more focused on the expectations and the opportunity," King says. And the 2013 T-shirt was unique in another respect. "It's the first red one," King says. "The others were black or grey. It was time for something different."

THE MEDIA, BOTH IN CANADA and across the United States, certainly sensed something different about the Blue Jays, not only because of their obvious infusion of talent but also because of their sundry story lines. R.A. Dickey, the erudite knuckleball pitcher, was the most prominent media target. Before he won the National League Cy Young Award in 2012, he had published a bestselling autobiography that chronicled his compelling saga of personal and professional redemption.

Dickey endured a tormented childhood. His mother was an alcoholic. His father was distant. As an eight year old, Dickey was sexually abused. He did not tell anyone until he was 32, and by then, both his personal life and baseball career were crumbling. "If I would've been left to my own devices, I would be dead," he says. Dickey conquered his personal demons with the help of a trusted counsellor, supportive family and friends, and his Christian faith. He saved his baseball career by learning to throw a knuckleball.

During the first week of spring training, a *60 Minutes* crew fronted by Lesley Stahl shadowed Dickey after visiting him at his home in Nashville and following him to Mumbai, where he spent several days in February helping to promote a clinic for victims of the sex trade. Early in 2011, he had climbed Mount Kilimanjaro to draw attention to the cause and raise money for the clinic. Now, back on the job in a new uniform in Dunedin, Dickey was a magnet for virtually every national baseball columnist in the U.S., as well as New York writers who had covered him with the Mets. As they toured spring-training sites, several of the best-known U.S. baseball writers visited Dunedin more than once to put their stamp on the story of the reborn pitcher and the reborn Blue Jays.

Generous with his time, Dickey often did one-on-one interviews early in the morning before workouts began, and again in the afternoon after they ended. Asked whether the media demands were onerous, he replied, "It doesn't feel irregular. It's not more than I can manage, I don't feel like. I mean, coming from New York certainly prepares you for that aspect."

The media rush continued, with Melky Cabrera's stilted news conference in which he declared that he had nothing to say about his 50-game suspension in 2012 for elevated testosterone levels, which forced him out of the San Francisco Giants lineup during their drive to a World Series championship. In addition, Tim Kurkjian and John Kruk of ESPN came to town and broadcast their show from a makeshift set behind the right-field wall; Jim Bowden of ESPN and SiriusXM radio did a show from Dunedin; and Ben McGrath of the *New Yorker* was among the legion of Dickey followers who made their way to the mundane ballpark known as Florida Auto Exchange Stadium.

Toronto media outlets also beefed up their coverage and devoted unprecedented resources and personnel to the Blue Jays. They reasoned that the 2013 team represented a chance that might not come again; at best, the team could spawn a new era of success for the franchise, heighten fan interest, and post record levels of advertising revenue. Sportsnet, the national sports network owned by Rogers Communications Inc., which also owns the Blue Jays, bet big on that outcome. The previous season, disappointing as it was, brought a 15 percent attendance boost. That momentum primed ownership to increase payroll, capitalize on the hype the new spending generated, and rake in the cash from new ticket purchases and spinoff sales.

"I think that we as a consolidated group knew that [in 2012] the Blue Jays were becoming fashionable again, so it all lined up for the timing to be perfect for [2013]," says Keith Pelley, president of Rogers Media. "Every year the Jays were becoming more fashionable and getting a stronger team, and every year Sportsnet's commitment was greater. This year it became evident that if we're going to spend the dollars, then we're going to increase our coverage that much more and our commitment that much more, and the better the Blue Jays do, the better Sportsnet does, and the better Sportsnet does, the better the Blue Jays do. So it really works hand in hand."

To that end, Sportsnet shipped a temporary set to Florida Auto Exchange Stadium and produced daily reports for its various news-update shows from there. Toronto all-sports radio station Sportsnet 590 The Fan broadcast a couple of its daily shows at the ballpark in two separate stints, while Sportsnet's website and magazine also churned out a steady stream of content. And then there was the marketing material generated inside the Car Wash, the nickname given to the temporary tent nearly half the size of a football field that was wedged into the team practice area beyond the stadium bleachers on the third-base side. The Car Wash housed a 25-by-25 foot stage, surrounded by two levels of scaffolding to support extras dressed as fans, a giant screen that many hockey arenas would envy, and the stadium lights central to the revised look of Blue Jays game broadcasts. Outside the tent were interview stations set up within the grungy visitors' clubhouse, plus a makeshift photo studio in a batting cage. Players were dragged through a gruelling two-day gauntlet of stops to create a bank of video, audio, and photo material for all arms of Rogers Media, including the Blue Jays, to use.

Nearly everyone on the scene — players, coaches, journalists, other media members, and crew — had never experienced anything like it. During a visit, club president Paul Beeston looked around and quipped, "I could have had two more players with what it cost to build this."

J.A. HAPP CAME WARY to spring training, and for good reason. Ever since he arrived in Toronto, via a summer 2012 trade with the Houston Astros, his experience was star-crossed. A career starter traded to the Blue Jays, a team with a fragile rotation, Happ was promptly banished to the bullpen. Four relief outings later, he became a starter again. After six starts, medical staff discovered his right foot was broken, likely the consequence of an awkward landing while covering first base in his penultimate start. Happ needed surgery. He was done for the season.

Back home in Chicago, Happ embarked on a tedious, taxing rehab program. Shortly after Happ started to walk again, Anthopoulos completed the Miami trade, which revamped the rotation overnight. The GM gave Happ a courtesy call. "He told me, 'As of right now you're our sixth starter. You'll be in there with probably seven or eight guys competing for jobs in the spring, and [you'll] either make the rotation, make the bullpen, or be optioned to Buffalo.'" Happ's reply? "I don't want to get into the details. He knows how I felt. I don't know what you say but how you feel and how you view yourself." He viewed himself as a major-league starter.

Speaking with reporters in late January, Anthopoulos left little doubt that Happ was destined for the opening-day start in Buffalo. Unless things changed. That was, and is, the GM's constant caveat: things change.

Happ did not accept his fate. He resented and worried about it, although publicly he was monotonously guarded and worked hard to bite his tongue. "It's certainly weighing on me a little bit," he acknowledged in a late-March understatement. In fact, it was weighing on him a lot, even as he was pitching well. Meanwhile, the anointed fifth starter, Ricky Romero, was a lost soul on the mound, still wearing the albatross of his dreadful 2012 season, his command and delivery mechanics unmanageable.

"Whatever happened last year, everyone has to just get over it,"

Romero said at one point. "It was bad, yeah, I know that, and I don't have to keep hearing it."

Therein lay the most compelling narrative of spring camp: a tale of two left-handers, one seeking justice, the other redemption. Eventually, this slow-moving plot exploded into a 48-hour denouement that left them both dumbfounded.

Spring statistics are notoriously unreliable, but Happ's were persuasive. In seven outings — all against American League East teams — he posted a 1.90 ERA. In four of those games he held opponents scoreless. But for most of his month of spring success, all signs pointed to him starting the season in Buffalo while Romero clung to the fifth starter's job in Toronto.

Romero, however, was making it difficult to sell that scenario. Undisputed staff ace in 2011 and opening-day starter in 2012, he had become a forlorn figure, abandoned by all the attributes that had made him a franchise cornerstone. His troubles persisted through spring training. The fan base once embraced Romero as a tough but soft-spoken East L.A. kid who never backed down on the mound and emerged as the team's top pitcher. Now that he was a faltering fifth starter, they turned heartlessly pragmatic. On merit, Happ had earned the job. Romero? Let him shuffle off to Buffalo.

For six weeks, management's narrative did not change: Romero is our fifth starter. Pitching coach Pete Walker, and Romero himself, gently scolded the media for making too much of his problems. Meanwhile, they worked behind the scenes to fix flaws in the pitcher's delivery mechanics — issues, they admitted, that had surfaced during his disastrous 2012 season. In 2011, Romero posted a 2.92 ERA and 15 wins. In 2012, his ERA was 5.77 — the worst among regular big-league starters — and only one of his nine wins came after June 22.

Romero also had walked 105 batters, the most in the majors. His inability to maintain a direct line to home plate undermined his control, but shortly after the season ended, two other factors emerged. After insisting all season that he was healthy, Romero underwent "minor" elbow surgery in mid-October. The team did not announce it until two weeks later. In a terse news release, the Blue Jays also revealed that Romero had received platelet-rich plasma (PRP) injections in both knees to address persistent tendinitis. The procedure involves withdrawing about 20 millilitres of a patient's blood, spinning it in a centrifuge to separate the components, then injecting the platelet-rich portion into the injured area to accelerate healing. Romero's knees burned so badly that he barely moved for two weeks.

Five months after the injections, Romero said he thought they'd had little effect. He continued to undergo regular therapy for his knees, but insisted they were fine and claimed his elbow was as good as new. His command problems persisted.

A turning point came on March 21 when he tested his revamped delivery against visiting Pittsburgh Pirates farmhands at the Jays' minor-league complex, a 10-minute drive from big-league camp. While Anthopoulos and his front-office lieutenants watched from behind home plate, Romero was hit hard by a bunch of callow minor-leaguers. He retired just seven batters and walked five. One of the Pirates' farmhands in the lineup that day told his agent that Romero looked "scared," and that "he had nothing" on the mound. Afterward, Anthopoulos said Romero would remain in the rotation, but wavered ever so slightly in his conviction. "The plans are the same," he said, "but just like anything else, you constantly evaluate."

Meanwhile, Happ maintained his edge as the best starting pitcher in camp. Finally, with less than a week left in spring training, Gibbons allowed that if he had his way, Happ would make the team as a long reliever. It seemed a utilitarian conclusion: if Romero struggled through short starts once the season started, at least Happ would be available to pitch three or four innings of relief while the offence fought back.

But Gibbons didn't tell Happ he had made the team. Meanwhile, Happ continued to seek answers from Anthopoulos. The GM said he had none to give. At work during the day, Happ managed to shut the door on his anxieties much of the time, except when reporters asked about them. But at home in the evening, they buzzed through his consciousness, leaving him to contemplate an apparent, and impending, injustice.

Ironically, behind the scenes, Happ's agent, Dave Rogers, and the Jays were negotiating a contract extension. Talks started late in spring training, and moved toward the finish line shortly after Romero suffered through that humiliating start against a Class-A team wearing Pirates uniforms.

Five days later, after another uneven start in a big-league exhibition game, Romero said he was making progress, and Gibbons said so, too. "I told him, 'Nice job,' and I saw him smile," Gibbons says. "I hadn't seen him smile in a while. He was putting a lot of pressure on himself. That tells me he felt pretty good."

The good feelings didn't last long. Late that afternoon, Anthopoulos convened a meeting to discuss the roster. Assistant GM Tony LaCava was there, along with Gibbons and Walker. Writers had just finished filing their stories on Romero's start when Jay Stenhouse, the club's vice-president of communications, burst into the Dunedin press box to announce that Anthopoulos would be available in 15 minutes to discuss a roster move.

Things had changed. Romero was going to the minors. "He's working on something that he hasn't completed yet, and we didn't have enough time to get him to complete it," Anthopoulos said. Romero would stay with the Class A Dunedin club for as long as he needed to iron out the kinks in his delivery. Happ was the new fifth starter.

The news rocked Romero. All spring, his bosses had stood behind him. Now Anthopoulos, LaCava, Gibbons, and Walker were telling him, as gently as they could, that the team was better off without him. "It was unanimous," Anthopoulos said. They also said they were confident he would work his way back, but there was no timeline.

The decision surprised some in the clubhouse, but for the most part, his teammates understood. One player lamented the way Romero approached the spring, believing he tried too hard to immediately show everybody he'd regained his form and was ready to make 2012 a thing of the past. "I feel like if he'd just gone through a gradual buildup, taking each step without worrying about results, and just trusting that in the end everything would be there, it might have turned out differently," the teammate said.

Two days later, in his first interview since his demotion, Romero stood in his new clubhouse at the minor-league complex, and revealed the roiling emotions he had experienced after his handlers delivered the news that kicked him in the gut and sent him into exile.

He could not admit that he was delusional when he cherry-picked hopeful signs from his final spring start. He could not accept that the technical flaws in his delivery represented the root of his problems.

"It's not mechanical," he insisted. "It's more just getting right mentally, getting that confidence and feeling right. I felt like after that last start there, I was feeling it again. And obviously then you get knocked down like that right after the game, it's something you don't expect. It hurts, and it hits me to the bottom of my heart, because I care so much and I've worked so hard for everything I have."

Whatever changes his bosses wanted, he vowed the process would be short. He had rented a new place in Toronto, had already shipped his belongings and his car to Canada, and would be there in a couple of weeks at most, he said.

He was wrong.

At the precise moment that Romero was talking to three reporters in minor-league camp, the rest of the media entourage was attending a news conference in major-league camp to announce Happ's new contract: two years, $8.9 million, with a $6.7 million team option for 2015. He still had minor-league options left. He even feared that if he pitched poorly the next day in his final exhibition start, he might still be sent down. He needn't have worried, but his lingering angst was understandable, given the drama that played out over recent months.

AS SPRING TRAINING WOUND DOWN, the roster that seemed so sound in mid-November was starting to show a few cracks. A nagging rib cage injury shut down Lawrie, who was hurt in a Team Canada exhibition game as he prepared for the World Baseball Classic. He would start the season on the disabled list. The Jays would carry eight relievers instead of the planned seven. The last two pitchers picked for the bullpen, Jeremy Jeffress and Brett Cecil, had posted spring ERAs of 7.62 and 6.61. Relievers Casey Janssen and Sergio Santos, each recovering from shoulder surgery, were still trying to convince management they could pitch effectively while carrying a normal workload that included appearances in back-to-back games. Gibbons abandoned his plan to use Adam Lind as the designated hitter against all comers. Lind would face right-handers, and perhaps the occasional lefty, but his longstanding difficulties against left-handers remained worrisome to those whose opinions mattered most.

And so much was new. Of the 25 players on this roster, 14 were not on the Blue Jays' 2012 opening-day roster. They opened the season with a new manager, a new hitting coach, a new pitching coach, a new first-base coach, and a new third-base coach. With so many people getting to know each other, building cohesion and trust would take time.

"I've been fortunate enough to be on some great teams, and on every one of those great teams there was never a problem with the guys in the clubhouse," says DeRosa, who played on eight teams that went to the post-season. "There was always a great, great chemistry and I don't think it gets enough credit. People write it off and say, 'Well, if you win, you have good chemistry and if you lose, you have bad chemistry.'

"I completely disagree with that. The manager sets the tone, but the clubhouse is ours. There are 25 players on the roster and if we don't enjoy being around each other, I don't care how good you are, eventually it will go south."

Every team starts a new season with question marks, and in relative terms, the Blue Jays did not look like a team in trouble. Most clubs would have willingly traded opening-day rosters with Toronto. In the eyes of most beholders, they had entered the elite ranks. A playoff berth was a near certainty. Among their fans, the excitement of November had risen to euphoria by the end of March.

And every day in the weight room, players saw an important reminder on the back of each other's red T-shirts. *Nothing is given. Everything is earned.*

The message would quickly hit home.

HOW QUICKLY
THINGS CHANGE:
ALEX ANTHOPOULOS

7

THE FIRST TORONTO BLUE JAYS game Alex Anthopoulos ever saw in person was Game 5 of the 1992 World Series against the Atlanta Braves. He was 15, a burgeoning baseball fan in a box seat, but he didn't consider it anything special. The Blue Jays were not his beloved Montreal Expos, after all, and he was nowhere near cognizant of the magnitude of what he was watching. This trip from his hometown of Montreal to Toronto was a lark. His buddy Mike Yermus had an uncle with a private box at the SkyDome, and invited Anthopoulos to come along. They drove down Highway 401, stayed overnight after the game — the boys played Sega Genesis games more than they slept — and returned home the next day. Lonnie Smith's fifth-inning grand slam off Jack Morris delayed the Blue Jays' champagne celebration for two nights, but Anthopoulos was neither deflated by the loss that evening nor jubilant over the eventual triumph in Atlanta. The Expos finished nine games back of the Pittsburgh Pirates in the National League East, and this wasn't his party.

"I followed the Blue Jays like I would any other team — casually," Anthopoulos recalls. "Everyone followed the Blue Jays when they were in the playoffs and World Series because it was a big deal, but it wasn't like, 'Oh my God, I can't believe I'm at a World Series, I can't believe I'm here to see the Blue Jays.' It was like, 'Yeah, it would be really cool to go, it'd be great.' But if it had been a team I was following for a long time, it would have been different . . . I didn't realize how special it was to be at the World Series, and how rare it was for a Canadian team."

Mike Yermus made Alex Anthopoulos a baseball fan. They met at Lower Canada College, a prestigious private school in Montreal. The Yermus family had season tickets for Expos games, and in 1992, Mike and Alex went to a lot of games at Olympic Stadium.

"I got into it heavily, and winning teams can bring that out of you," he says. "For me it was more 1992 when I started to really, really get the bug, when [manager] Felipe Alou came on board, and the Expos started playing better. All of a sudden it was a contending team, a competitive team, and it's a lot easier to follow. That's when I really got into it, and then every year it grew because the team kept getting better and it climaxed in 1994 when they were playing great."

The Expos looked like the class of baseball that year until an August players strike killed the season, and since then, there hasn't been a sniff of post-season baseball in Canada. But thanks to that kid from Montreal, once indifferent to the Blue Jays' plight, and the extraordinary off-season deals he managed to pull off leading into 2013, Toronto fans regarded the end of that drought as a given by the time spring training wrapped up. Anthopoulos had completed a highly unlikely ascension to general manager in Toronto three and a half years earlier, and his work drew kudos all around. Before the Blue Jays had even played a game in 2013, oddsmakers made them 3-1 favourites to win the American League East and 7-1 choices to win the World Series. In a *Toronto Star* fan poll, 89 percent of respondents predicted a trip to the playoffs. The regular season had become an inconvenience to be tolerated until the real fun started.

Players, too, were locked into that belief.

"The sky is the limit for us because I know how many good players we have," Jose Bautista told reporters as camp opened February 12. "This is by far the best team I've played on. I just don't see where it can go bad for us. Because of those reasons I think we should, and we could, be in the playoffs and the World Series."

ALEX ANTHOPOULOS BARELY PLAYED baseball as a kid. His Greek-immigrant father preached education to his three sons and hoped they would join him in the family heating and ventilation business. His music-mad boys, however, were more interested in heating and ventilating their basement with covers of Led Zeppelin. Aside from a casual interest in the Montreal Canadiens, the Anthopoulos family cared little for sports.

John Anthopoulos did all he could to stir his sons' interest in the wonders of heating and ventilation. Walking through a mall, he would direct young Alex's eyes to the ceiling. "See that? See that?" he would say, beholding a trail of ductwork as though it were a Henry Moore sculpture. He brought home blueprints, spread them out, and gathered the boys around. "It was the most boring thing in the world," Alex says.

But it gave the family a life they could not have enjoyed in Greece. John was born in Omonoia, about 25 minutes outside of Athens, but immigrated to Canada in search of a better life, earned an engineering degree from McGill, and started a successful business. Alex was the youngest of three sons raised in Montreal's tony Westmount neighbourhood. Education and hard work were hallmarks of their upbringing, but music was their passion. They jammed together in the basement, with George, the eldest, on guitar, Billy on drums, and Alex on bass. They made eight-track recordings.

Of the brothers, George pursued music most vigorously. His father warned that George was destined to busk for change in subway terminals. "You're going to have your case open, and we'll come and we'll scoop the change,'" Alex remembers his father saying, a barb meant to hammer home the message: "Make sure you do something responsible with your life, because how many people make it?" But George made it. He studied music at Concordia and now teaches it at an Italian school in Montreal. Billy, however, was the family's truly gifted musician, Alex says. Though he never pursued music full-time, Billy became an accomplished drummer, playing on Sam Roberts' 2006 album *Chemical City*. He's also a licensed pilot, but has made a career in real estate. His father's admonitions may have affected Billy the most, Alex believes: "He wanted a profession."

Alex was much less certain about what he wanted. Music was his primary hobby in high school. After enrolling at LCC in grade three, he joined the music program in grade eight and travelled with the school band to Memphis, New Orleans, and Chicago. Then he met Mike Yermus in a grade seven French class, and in 1992 they watched the Expos finish second with a roster that included Larry Walker, Gary Carter, and Dennis Martinez. Alex and Mike also played on the same baseball team for two years. Alex was a catcher but recalls having to pitch once after Mike, their pitcher, got ejected from a game. "I did okay," he says. It was the only time the future general manager ever played the sport.

After Alex enrolled as a business student at McMaster University, he became obsessed with sports, again thanks to the influence of another friend, Rich Martinelli, a dorm neighbour who lived and breathed sports. As a mundane life in heating and ventilation loomed over him, Alex dreamed of an exciting career in the sports industry.

POWERED BY THE CITY'S four newspapers and the Sportsnet media machine, Blue Jays mania swept Toronto in the weeks leading up to the start of the 2013 season. When opening night arrived, there were more reporters than players on the field during batting practice. Nearly 49,000 fans filled the Rogers Centre, shaking the girders with their cheers during the player introductions. Prominent among the newly arrived heroes was starter R.A. Dickey, who, two days earlier, had climbed the pitcher's mound in the empty stadium and thrown a few pitches. "It's a nice place to throw a knuckleball," he declared, joining the parade of optimists.

Far more cautious in both his public and private predictions was Anthopoulos, who spent the winter and early part of spring ducking the "genius" tag fans kept trying to pin on him, and the "favourite" label so many tried to stick on his team. The massive hype troubled him. "I just think it's disrespectful to your opponents," he says. "The whole 'Look at us,' it just doesn't feel right. People were saying World Series favourites and it was like, 'Whoa, did all these other teams vanish?'"

But there was no room for logic or rationale, and the team's arrival in Toronto from spring training felt like a coronation. While some players marvelled at the hoopla, some found it annoying, and others embraced the attention as a sign the Blue Jays had finally arrived as true contenders. "There's that quieter confidence, where you're not trying to trick yourself into believing you're going to be able to do it," said Brandon Morrow. "Last year we were hopefully optimistic. This year we expect to win. There's a little bit of a quiet confidence or swagger, where you just feel like this is the team put together to win."

They did not win on opening night, nor on Day 2. And after a victory to avoid a sweep against the Cleveland Indians, they lost two of the next three to the Boston Red Sox, whose manager, John Farrell, inspired resounding boos upon his return to the Rogers Centre. The Blue Jays were 2-4 out of the gate before hitting the road. During the 3-3 trip that followed, Jose Reyes suffered a sprained left ankle that would sideline him until June 26, and Morrow's nagging arm problems began to surface. The snowball continued to build, and after a 3-4 homestand against the feeble Chicago White Sox and makeshift New York Yankees, the Blue Jays buried themselves with a 1-6 showing through Baltimore and the Bronx. Manager John Gibbons called a brief team meeting following a loss to the Yankees on April 19 in Toronto, while veteran Mark DeRosa convened a players-only session on April 28 before the team lost again in Yankee Stadium.

A victory over the Red Sox on April 30 finished the 10-17 month on a somewhat optimistic note, but panic had already set in. Vocal portions of the fan base and the media demanded changes. Some critics sought simplistic solutions — an absurd daily discussion demanded the Jays bring up minor-league journeyman Jim Negrych, who was hitting up a storm at Triple-A Buffalo, to play second base. #FireGibby turned into a trendy and, ultimately, season-long Twitter hashtag for the disenfranchised. All the background noise prompted the Blue Jays to cloister themselves from outside fears that the roof was caving in on a dream season. Caught in the crucible was Anthopoulos, whose bold off-season moves were designed to make dreams come true, not shatter them. He preached patience and faith while trying to block out the hysteria.

"A big part of it, and I told myself this even in the off-season," he explains, "was I wouldn't read or follow things [in the media], because your emotions can be influenced, and it won't help me." Returning from a road trip, someone told him that Maple Leaf Sports and Entertainment had hired Tim Leiweke as CEO. It was a big story in Toronto sports circles, but it wasn't until well after the fact that it was news to Anthopoulos. "Where have you been?" Beeston asked. "I said, 'Paul, I haven't been reading, I haven't been doing anything. I've just been with the team.' That's how much I was in my own little world. And I had to do that."

BACK HOME FOR THE SUMMER after his second year at McMaster, Alex went out for lunch with his father one Tuesday afternoon. Alex sensed something wasn't right. "I'm tired," his dad said. "I'm not going to go back to the office. I'm just going to go home." Alex had never heard his father talk that way before. Later that night, John Anthopoulos booked an appointment with a cardiologist for the next day, and during that exam learned he had suffered a heart attack and needed to check in to the hospital immediately. Bypass surgery was scheduled for the next week.

During a visit that night, Anthopoulos traded jokes with his father in his room at Royal Victoria Hospital. There seemed no cause for worry. But while awaiting the bypass operation, on Friday, May 15, 1998, with son Billy by his side, he suffered a massive heart attack in his hospital bed. Moments later, he was dead.

Alex got the news while at work at his father's business. "Billy called me. 'Dad just started going into a heart attack.' He was panicking," Anthopoulos recalls. "I was like, 'Call me back' and hung up the phone. In between Mike Yermus called me. I remember I was sitting in a boardroom at the office, and [Mike] said, 'Mike Piazza got traded.' My head was in the clouds, spinning, and I just said, 'Mike, I can't talk right now.' After that Billy called me back and said, 'He's gone.'"

Exactly 10 days away from his 21st birthday, Anthopoulos was too stunned to cry. All he wanted to do was go home. Once there, he rushed to meet Jeannine St. Hilaire, the caregiver who became like a second mother to him and his brothers after his parents divorced when he was 11.

"I jumped in her arms and was just bawling," he says.

Soon after his father's sudden death, Anthopoulos decided the worst thing he could do with his life was to spend it at a job he absolutely hated. And he absolutely hated running the family business, which he and his brothers took over after the funeral. "When he died it was like, 'We have to continue on,'" he says.

Anthopoulos returned to McMaster for his third year, trying to run the company at the same time. He was miserable. "I remember whining to Rich Martinelli, 'Man, I'd really love to be in sports,'" Anthopoulos says. "We were sitting on a bus and he said, 'Jesus, I'm sick of hearing you talk about it. Just do it.'" But instead, he dropped out of school and returned to Montreal to focus on the family business, enrolling in night classes at Montreal's Vanier College to try to get a handle on the technical side of heating and ventilation. He worked for two years before he and his brothers had enough. "We were like, 'I'm not doing this for the next 40 years of my life,'" he says. The business had been built on their father's expertise and connections. "We weren't engineers, we hadn't taken any engineering, so we decided to sell it. We didn't get a whole lot."

The main benefit of the sale was a newfound freedom to pursue whatever they wanted. The shock of his father's sudden death made Anthopoulos realize that a dream delayed could mean a dream unfulfilled. His dream was to work in baseball. So in 2000, at age 23, Anthopoulos started calling big-league teams, eventually mustering the courage to phone then–Expos GM Jim Beattie. The first time, Anthopoulos hung up before the call went through. The second time, he offered to do anything, for free. He started by sorting fan mail, working part-time at a bank to help support himself, and eventually moved up to a $7 per hour gig in public relations, photocopying game notes and doing other gopher work. During games, he sat in the stands and relentlessly pestered scouts with questions. Expos head scout Fred Ferreira took notice, and eventually brought Anthopoulos to his baseball camp in Florida for another unpaid internship, helping his curious charge learn the ins and outs of scouting and grading players. The team he loved as a teenager soon hired him as an assistant in international scouting, then promoted him to coordinator of scouting operations in 2002. The next year, they added Canadian scouting supervisor to his title. He was 26.

THE LASTING APRIL IMAGE of the 2013 Blue Jays is that of Jose Reyes in a heap at second base, holding his left ankle, tears streaking his cheeks. It was April 12 at Kauffman Stadium in Kansas City, and the Blue Jays were in the midst of a rally that would lock up a victory. Having just delivered a two-run single, Reyes tried to steal second base. On his way, he shot a quick look toward the plate. Thinking Melky Cabrera had struck out, he broke stride slightly, then saw the catcher's throw zooming toward the bag.

Trapped in no man's land, Reyes tried an awkward slide even though he was perilously close to the bag. His left ankle got caught under his body and twisted violently as his weight came down upon it. As the TV cameras captured his portrait of pain, fans needed no medical expertise to know Reyes was in serious trouble. His grimace and tears foreshadowed the formal diagnosis: a severe ankle sprain, requiring roughly three months of recovery and rehabilitation to repair torn ligaments.

After losing three consecutive series, the Blue Jays had lost their star shortstop and leadoff hitter, carted off the field in a utility vehicle and later rolled out of the stadium in a wheelchair. "It's a nightmare," Gibbons said.

The next day Munenori Kawasaki arrived as Reyes' short-term replacement. Meanwhile, Anthopoulos worked the phones, finding the asking price for Brendan Ryan of the Seattle Mariners and John McDonald of the Pittsburgh Pirates obscenely high. Before long, Kawasaki would grow into a local cult hero and beloved clubhouse presence, but the quirky antics that made the eccentric Japanese spark-plug so popular did little to mask both his and the club's deficiencies, particularly the vaunted starting rotation that had been hyped as the team's backbone.

In 27 April games, Blue Jays starters earned only five wins. While the "win" stat is widely considered a poor measure of performance, in this instance it underlined how infrequently the starters pitched deep into games, often leaving with their team on the losing end of the score. With the starters averaging just over five innings per game, the Jays were constantly playing catch-up, and often, the sluggish offence could not overcome the deficit the starter created.

Dickey averaged six innings in six starts, winning just twice with an ERA of 4.50. Brandon Morrow was winless in six starts with a 5.29 ERA. Mark Buehrle was 1-1 with a 6.35 ERA in five starts, and Josh Johnson was 0-1 with a 6.86 ERA in four. J.A. Happ, slated to open the season either in the bullpen or at Triple-A Buffalo, led the starters with a 3.86 ERA while posting a 2-1 record in five starts.

More troubling were the health issues, both lingering and looming. Pitching with muscle spasms in his right shoulder blade, Dickey lost velocity and late bite on his knuckleball. Johnson skipped his April 26 start at Yankee Stadium with a triceps issue that would send him to the disabled list in early May and cost him a month. And Morrow's right arm was like a ticking time bomb.

Morrow's season debut April 3 was something to behold: eight strikeouts in six innings and 98s routinely popping up on the radar gun. He simply overwhelmed the Cleveland Indians. Hopped up on first-start adrenaline, the right-hander suffered a forearm flexor strain in that game. "The effort level he pitched at was insane," one club executive said. "He was pitching like it was Game 7 of the World Series." In his next start, on a frigid afternoon in Detroit, Morrow struggled through pain and failed to make it out of the fourth inning. On April 14, he held the Royals to a pair of runs over six innings in what ended as a 3-2 loss. Pitching at 90–91 mph, he felt like his elbow was about to explode on each pitch. The soreness eased for a while, but after starting in April's finale against the Red Sox, allowing three runs and striking out seven in five innings, Morrow would make just four more starts before he landed on the disabled list. The initial diagnosis was a forearm strain but the pain was different than before. Ultimately, tests revealed an entrapped radial nerve in his forearm. His season was over.

Complicating matters was an all-or-nothing offence that batted .231 in April with an on-base percentage of .294. Though the Blue Jays hit 35 home runs in the month, they averaged just 3.85 runs per game and too often came up a key hit short. After the Yankees swept them in New York, Gibbons was asked what he could do to help out his offence. "You want me to go out there and hit or something?" he replied testily. "I couldn't hit when I played, how am I going to do it now?" By then, #FireGibby was entrenched as the panacea sought by social media's torch and pitchfork set looking for easy answers, the level of discourse devolving by the day. Despite the frustrations, Gibbons took it in stride. "That's fair, I've got no problem with that," he said of the calls for his head. "That's usually always the first target, but I can live with that, I've been in this seat before. We're playing close games, we're just not winning any of them. Eventually we will. I understand their frustrations. They don't have any more frustration than we've got, I'll tell you that."

EACH STEP THROUGH HIS early apprenticeship with the Expos, Anthopoulos impressed his supervisors, whether by asking Major League Baseball's Scouting Bureau for video of thousands of amateur players to watch in his spare time, or by breaking down players' skills with club scouting director Dana Brown, trying to glean any bit of insight he could. A vivid memory for Brown is how, in the lead-up to the 2002 draft, Anthopoulos kept pushing for the Expos to take Prince Fielder with the fifth overall pick. He lost the argument, Brown instead selecting right-hander Clint Everts, who has yet to break past Triple-A. Fielder, a five-time all-star, went seventh to the Milwaukee Brewers, after the Royals picked future Cy Young Award winner Zack Grienke. "That's one of the lessons you learn as a scouting director," says Brown, now a special assistant to Anthopoulos with the Blue Jays. "Sometimes you never know where the truth is coming from."

As much as Anthopoulos loved the Expos, he could read the writing on the wall about their bleak future and jumped ship after the 2003 season to join the Blue Jays as a scouting coordinator. His star quickly rose. The Jays promoted him to assistant general manager at the end of the 2005 season and added vice-president, baseball operations to his title in 2006. Amid handling contracts and arbitration cases — former GM J.P. Ricciardi used to call him The Barracuda because of the way he dealt with agents, praising him for being able to "talk a starving dog out of a steak" — Anthopoulos also developed a close relationship with Paul Beeston, who maintained an office in the Blue Jays executive suites after he left the team to serve as Major League Baseball's chief operating officer. Beeston paid rent; he didn't want any favours. But after he returned from New York, he was available. After all, the gregarious, cigar-chomping Beeston was the Blue Jays' very first employee in 1976; no one else with the club had his institutional memory and his connections across baseball, among them commissioner Bud Selig. "I have an ear with Buddy boy," he says.

Beeston's office was at the west end of the Blue Jays executive suites, and Anthopoulos regularly stopped by to pick his brain. "Where the fuck did he come from?" Beeston remembers asking Jon Lalonde, the Blue Jays scouting director who had lured Anthopoulos from the Expos. "It was quite obvious this guy was unique," Beeston says. "I sensed that the first day I met him."

In 2008, Beeston took over from Paul Godfrey as Blue Jays president and CEO on an interim basis, charged with running the club while finding his own replacement. At that point the team was already in decline, and by season's end, a near revolt had formed in the clubhouse against manager Cito Gaston. Ricciardi was fired on the penultimate day of the 2009 season, replaced by the 33-year-old Anthopoulos. Beeston emphasized that it was not an interim appointment. "Alex was a no-brainer for me," he says. "I hadn't seen something like this in a long, long time, in business, forget baseball. He hit the ground running that first day and never went to sleep, I'm convinced."

The franchise underwent a dramatic makeover on both the business and baseball sides. Beeston overhauled everything from the way tickets were sold to accounting procedures. Anthopoulos reinvested in scouting and player development, and traded Roy Halladay and Vernon Wells, clearing the deck for a new generation of players. The millions of new dollars the Blue Jays spent in the draft and in Latin America set the stage for the blockbusters with the Marlins and Mets that gave the team, at long last, a legitimate shot at a championship.

AT MARK DEROSA'S PLAYERS-ONLY meeting, Jose Bautista, R.A. Dickey, and Darren Oliver also spoke, each bothered by a growing fatalism among their teammates, a tendency to give away at-bats, and an inability to pick up each other. "You can't help but see the vibe of the whole dugout and whole clubhouse kind of waiting for something bad to happen," DeRosa explained afterward. "That's just human nature. We have too good a rotation, too good a lineup for that to be the norm. I felt like give it a month and see what happens, but I felt it was a situation that needed to be addressed."

After the meeting, the Blue Jays lost 3-2, capping a four-game Yankees sweep. They had dropped 10 of their past 13 games.

As he mentioned repeatedly during the season, DeRosa felt it was unfair for Gibbons to shoulder all the blame for the team's shortcomings.

"I think we needed to come together and not have to have it be Gibby all the time calling us together . . . We've got too good a club to just accept the position we're in and just see what happens. I don't want to just see what happens. Like I told the guys, I didn't come back [from near-retirement] to see what happens, I came back because this roster offered me a chance to get back to the post-season, and everyone should feel that way. You can't leave it up to Gibby and the coaching staff every time."

Nine days earlier in Toronto, Gibbons had called his own team meeting, trying to rally his players after a 9-4 loss to the Yankees. It lasted only a couple of minutes, his message a simple one: relax, play smarter, and trust that the wins will come.

Privately, that's what Anthopoulos was thinking too. "I don't know if I would have done this four years ago, but you know that you have no choice but to ride it out," he says. "From an offensive standpoint we didn't hit at all, and if you look at 2012, it was the same thing. We had the best starters' ERA for two months and they kept us in the game and we were around .500. So I'd been through it before. I'd been through Bautista hitting .180. I remember talking to Gibby about it at one point and saying, 'Watch.'"

Nothing was going right. But it was early.

"Everybody in the lineup was cold other than Reyes, and then we lost Reyes. Defensively, everyone was playing poorly, and you had all these guys with career track records that had done it, and it's just like making an evaluation in spring training. Sometimes it's amazing how quickly things change."

The 2009 season taught him to distrust small sample sizes. On May 18 that year, the Blue Jays were the league's top team with a 27-14 record. They finished 12 games under .500.

Early in '09, "I bought into it, totally," Anthopoulos says. "We just kept winning, six weeks, 27-14. We go on the road, we lose nine in a row, and from the middle of May to the end of the season we were third-worst in the game. So I'd seen the other side of it."

That's why, in 2013, he felt he had reason to believe in another kind of turnaround.

"Are all these starters going to have 6.00 ERAs? Really good chance that they're not," he says. "Are all these guys going to hit .180, .210? Probably not. The tough part is riding it out. And the way we were set up, you didn't have a choice but to ride it out, and it's unfortunate, you're putting yourself in a hole, all that kind of stuff. But panicking would be the worst thing you could do."

Which is not to say he folded his arms, sat back, and simply waited for better days. Anthopoulos constantly consulted with his front-office aides, with Gibbons and the coaches, and with the players themselves, asking questions, seeking solutions, trying to boost their confidence. All along, a single conviction kept his own confidence up.

"We were clearly going to be better," he says.

IN THE CROSSHAIRS: JOSE BAUTISTA

8

FANS IN TORONTO HAVE an unhealthy history of building up their sports stars, praising them intensely during their peak, and then turning on them when disappointment over the seemingly inevitable failure to deliver a championship reaches a crescendo. When things go bad, they tend to eat their own. At the beginning of May 2013, Jose Bautista seemed headed for the same treatment that had chewed up some of the city's other recent athletic icons — Carlos Delgado, Vernon Wells, Mats Sundin, and Chris Bosh. Roy Halladay is among the precious few to have avoided the backlash, even after forcing his trade from the Toronto Blue Jays, tying Alex Anthopoulos's hands with his no-trade clause in the process. Significant swaths of the fan base still regard Doc as a saint, his desire to move on accepted and understood. They blamed the team. Bautista, signed through 2015 with an option for 2016, wasn't getting nearly as much rope, despite being an elite slugger with a team-friendly contract and being one of the foundational pillars the Blue Jays were built on.

After a 10-1 loss to the Boston Red Sox to open May, Bautista's batting average dropped to .195, although his OBP was a comparatively healthy .311 with a .519 slugging percentage. Still, some fans had questioned his manhood in an appalling fashion via social media earlier in the season, when ankle and back injuries forced him from the lineup, while others summarily labelled him a hothead prone to harmful outbursts directed at umpires. His money quote from the second day of the season about his emotional interactions with the men in black — "Sometimes I have trouble more than other players dealing with my production being affected by somebody else's mediocrity" — became fodder for columnists across the continent. The common theme: Bautista was costing himself calls through selfish behaviour. Frustrated fans looking for scapegoats ran with the narrative, disinterested in facts. His back flared up when he volunteered to play third base for a pair of games in the wake of the Jose Reyes injury. The spasms were so bad that sitting down was sometimes a challenge. Meanwhile, instability in the ankle he turned while beating a double-play relay kept him from comfortably generating full power in his violent and fearsome swing. None of that mattered. The mob ruled: Bautista wasn't a leader. "If that's my weakness as a player, then I guess I must be doing all right in other aspects," he said of the furor over his outbursts. "I wish everybody else was more concerned about other things that I'm not doing right on the field, and not the way I react to umpires."

Jose Bautista is not a hothead. Fiery? Sure. Intense? Definitely. Aggressive? Without a doubt. But he's not a loose cannon, running around out of control, the way he was perceived to be at times during the 2013 season. That was an oversimplified, one-dimensional characterization of someone far deeper and more complex.

IF NOT FOR HIS thunderous swing and laser-beam throws from right field, Bautista might have ended up a money manager or venture capitalist. Before settling with the Pittsburgh Pirates for $500,000 on May 19, 2001 — an outstanding bonus for a 20th-round draft pick — Bautista had signed a letter of intent with the University of South Carolina, choosing the Gamecocks over similar offers from Miami, Georgia, LSU, and Tulane. Why? "Not only was South Carolina one of the best [baseball] programs at the time," Bautista explains, "but they had one of the best business schools in the nation." He planned to focus on finance. He wasn't going to major in baseball.

That emphasis on education was drilled into Bautista and younger brother Luis by parents Americo, who ran a poultry farm, and Sandra, an accountant for a large conglomerate, in their middle-class Santo Domingo home in the Dominican Republic. The family vacationed in Puerto Rico and Miami, the boys attended a private school, and home-work always came before home runs. Bautista excelled at math and the sciences, and he picked up English in class and from TV. "We always had cable growing up, so I watched baseball and the same shows as any American kid," he says. "From watching, I learned a lot and that kept my English up to date." He excelled at baseball, too, but as a speedy, line-drive hitter, not the slugger he'd eventually become. Rafael Perez, a key figure on Bautista's atypical path to the big leagues, remembers "a great outfielder, good arm, ran well. A gap-to-gap guy." Adds Perez, now Major League Baseball's director of Dominican operations, "He had quick wrists and quick hands. But if you asked me if he would have the power he has, I'd say no."

Bautista grew up playing in multiple leagues to fill his week with as much baseball as possible. One league played on Wednesdays and Fridays and was run by Perez's father, Oscar, another critical con-nection who, even after his own league closed down, kept close tabs on the young Bautista. Another league run by Abraham Mejia — now a player agent working with Paul Kinzer, who represents Edwin Encarnacion — practised on Mondays and played games on Saturday. Emilio Bonifacio also played in that loop but was a couple of years behind Bautista. Finally, there was Francisco Cordero's league, which played on Sundays. "I liked baseball," says Bautista, "and as long as I did my homework, my parents let me do it." As he got older, he shifted to another city league run by Enrique "Quique" Cruz (whose daughter, Carolina, is married to Pedro Martinez), where he continued to gain notice. Still, studies never took a back seat to baseball, which is why, unlike the majority of Dominican big-leaguers, he didn't leave home at a young age in the hope of signing professionally when first eligible at 16. "That wasn't even a thought in my house. I wouldn't even dare to bring it up," he says. "There was no way they would allow me to drop out of school to pursue baseball, so I had to figure out a way to do both. That was the only way."

By the time he graduated from high school in 1998, Bautista's potential as a baseball player earned him several opportunities. The New York Yankees invited him to their Dominican Republic academy that fall, at the same time Bautista was enrolled in business classes at Pontificia Universidad Catolica Madre y Maestra. "I would either take public transportation or my dad would drop me off at the Yankees complex," he says. "I had to be there at 7 a.m., but that wasn't terribly far from my house. I would go every day and work out there, and then at night I'd go to college 6 to 10, wake up, and do it all over again." After three months there, the Yankees offered $5,000 for him to sign. No chance. Next he worked out with the Arizona Diamondbacks, whose head of Latin American operations, Junior Noboa, liked Bautista a lot more. He'd pick up Bautista every morning at the side of the road that led from Santo Domingo to the facility in Boca Chica, about 40 minutes away, and then drop him off at night. Eventually he offered roughly $60,000, but again Bautista said no, equating the amount of money a team was willing to invest in him with the number and quality of opportunities he'd get in the farm system. The smaller the bonus, he figured, the easier for a club to cut its losses and move on. "I came from a different place than where some of these kids come from," he says. "I had open doors and opportunities if I pursued an education. I could get a good job if I graduated from college, I could get those internships, I could work and study and make a living, and probably make more money than I was being offered to become a professional baseball player at the time. Some of these kids wouldn't have those opportunities."

Yet baseball was the dream, so in spring 1999 Bautista attended a Team One prospect showcase event in St. Petersburg, Florida — Prince Fielder was among the other attendees — to get some fresh eyes on him. The Cincinnati Reds liked what they saw and invited him to their complex in the Dominican. Eventually they offered him $300,000, and Bautista was ready to accept but the contract was pulled once ownership of the franchise changed hands from Marge Schott to Carl Lindner. "It never became real," says Bautista, who was suddenly stuck in no man's land again. "I was actually just planning to not play anymore because I had no other options. Being close to turning 19 as a free agent in the Dominican Republic, I'm not going to get any significant offers."

That was not only true of big-league teams, but also American colleges willing to pony up scholarships. In between his studies and workouts, Bautista made VHS demo tapes of himself that he sent to various baseball coaches in the U.S. "It was just hell," he says of the entire process, and that was before his pitches went unanswered. One of the few nibbles he did get was from Jacksonville University, "but they said they had no scholarship money, they'd take me on as a walk-on." For an international student at the private school, tuition would have been about $40,000 a year before living expenses, a total no-go for Bautista after his family fell on some hard times. Hurricane Georges, which tore through the Dominican Republic in 1998 and caused about $1 billion in damage, wiped out his father's poultry farming business, and his mother had taken ill and was unable to work for a period of time. Hence, Bautista felt that his window of opportunity was closing, and that it might be time to focus exclusively on his business studies.

Then, an unlikely chain of events began, ultimately leading Bautista to the big leagues. It started with Oscar Perez, the man who had run one of the kids' leagues he played in, tipping off his son Rafael about Bautista. The junior Perez was a graduate of the Latin Athletes Education Fund, a program created by American businessman Don Odermann that helped connect qualified students with partial or full scholarships in American colleges, and provided money to cover short-falls for books, food, computers, and other necessities. In gratitude to Odermann, Perez and Juan Peralta, another fund graduate, kept an eye out for potential candidates and took note of Bautista while he worked out with the Diamondbacks, making sure to follow his progress. Not long after Bautista's deal with the Reds fell through, Peralta went to the United States in a bid to place an infielder at one of the colleges on his itinerary. While at Chipola Junior College in the Florida panhandle town of Marianna, coach Jeff Johnson told Peralta he had plenty of infielders, but needed an outfielder. "I told him I've got an outfielder, his name is Jose Bautista, he's already passed the TOEFL [Test of English as a Foreign Language] and has very good high-school grades," says Peralta, now the Dominican Republic academy director for the Reds. "I gave him a scouting report on the baseball side. The coach said, 'I'll go by your word, I trust you, so I'm going to give him a full ride.'"

Peralta and Perez called Bautista with the news and "within five days I was gone," money from Odermann helping cover financial gaps in his scholarship. It was a gift he never forgot, and when Odermann's failing health essentially mothballed the Latin Athletes Education Fund over the past couple of years, Bautista launched his own foundation, the Bautista Family Education Fund, to fill the void. Perez and Peralta both serve on the board. "He told me one time, 'I want to take advantage of what I am right now to really make an impact.' That really earned my respect even more," says Perez. "He's very much aware that the time he has as [a prominent player] is limited. It's not going to last forever, even though he's building a name that will hopefully carry on after his career is over. He knows this is the time when he has to take advantage of trying to do this, because a lot of people will do things just because of who he is, and that right there says a lot about him."

THE FIRST REAL SIGN of life for the Blue Jays in 2013 came on May 6 in St. Petersburg, Florida, when they fell behind 7-0 early but eventually rallied for a gripping 8-7 victory over the Tampa Bay Rays. While Bautista wasn't front and centre in the box score, despite having two hits, a walk, and a late sacrifice fly that cut the deficit to one run, the tenacious and professional at-bats he took throughout the game set the tone for his team, right up to J.P. Arencibia's game-winning two-run shot in the ninth. The next night, when the Blue Jays had to push aside the frightening sight of J.A. Happ taking a screaming line drive off his head, and fight back from a 4-1 deficit, Bautista delivered an RBI double in the eighth inning that tied the score in what ended as a 6-4 victory. The following Sunday at Fenway Park he hit a pair of home runs in a 12-4 thrashing of the Red Sox that gave the Blue Jays two of three in Boston and just their second series win of the season. On May 22, Bautista drove in all four runs in a 4-3 victory at home over the Rays, tying the score in the ninth with a solo shot off Fernando Rodney and winning it in the 10th with an opposite-field single off Cesar Ramos. That handed the Blue Jays another series win against an AL East rival. Having seemingly bottomed out at 13-24 after being one-hit by Jon Lester and the Red Sox on May 10, the tide appeared to have turned, even after the injury to Happ and the quickly aborted return of

Ricky Romero from his minor-league exile after just two starts. But as would become a theme for the season, the momentum didn't last long. During the Jays' four-game split with Baltimore at home toward the end of the month, the Orioles chewed up and spit out prospect Sean Nolin in a messy six-run, 1.1 inning big-league debut. The same series triggered a period of turmoil for Brett Lawrie that didn't end until he landed on the disabled list with an ankle sprain.

On the night Nolin made his debut, Lawrie stumbled into controversy with an umpire after grumbling about a couple of strike calls by Dan Bellino, slamming his helmet to the ground after striking out, and then getting ejected for tossing his batting gloves toward home plate as he walked away. "From my standpoint, the at-bat was over, flipped my bat down, flipped my helmet down, and walked to my position. Apparently you get in trouble for that," said a frustrated Lawrie. He insisted he had done nothing wrong. "I didn't say one word to [Bellino] — not one. Didn't look at him one time, and I'm in trouble for that." While there was some understanding for Lawrie in the clubhouse afterward, there was none two days later, when he stared down and yelled at Adam Lind and third base coach Luis Rivera when Lind didn't score on Lawrie's fly ball in the ninth inning. Both Gibbons and Bautista pounced on Lawrie in the dugout as soon as he returned. "Everybody noticed it was out of place and that's why both of us said something to him," Bautista said. Had Munenori Kawasaki not delivered the game-winning two-run double — and the post-game interview with Sportsnet's Arash Madani during which he famously proclaimed, "I am JAH-PAH-NEEEEESE!" — the turmoil would have been even more front and centre.

Lawrie apologized to his teammates the next day, after lengthy chats with Bautista, Gibbons, and DeRosa, who served as guidance counsellor to the third baseman all year. "There's no hard feelings for anybody," Lind said afterward, but there were some deeper concerns about Lawrie's behaviour. "I know how terrible Brett feels about it, that's what he's saying, what he feels, but you can only do it so many times before you have to look in the mirror and realize you're the one making the mistakes consistently," said one player. "Where we're at as a team, it's got to be all about winning . . . His heart is in right place, he cares about the guys. Sometimes he needs to be reminded about handling himself a certain way."

Later that night Lawrie turned his ankle sliding into second base on a steal attempt. A couple of days later he was on the disabled list with a sprain that would cost him a month. The wild stretch in which Lawrie snapped at umpires and teammates alike turned the Canuck's manic style of play into a polarizing talking point, and all of a sudden Lawrie was the new lightning rod, with Bautista the voice of reason. "His intensity is what makes him good," Bautista said. "I don't think he should not play with intensity or dial it down." And showing up a teammate and coach on the field? "It was addressed," said Bautista. "I don't think it will be a problem going forward."

BAUTISTA, BETTER THAN MOST, understands the constant struggle to channel such uber-intensity in a positive direction. For as long as he can remember, he's played with a similar fire. "If I don't have that, I'm not the same player," he says. "I need that for sure." At the same time he concedes, "There are very rare instances where it works against me, but I have tried to keep working at getting better at channelling that energy in a better way." Much of that struggle occurred with the Pittsburgh Pirates, who insisted that Bautista, a natural pull-hitter, slap the ball to the opposite field. (To this day he continues to chafe at the suggestion, even though he did go the other way to beat defensive shifts a handful of times in 2013.) He also had a tough time coping with failure. In his 51st game with Single-A Lynchburg in 2003, his third season of pro ball, he broke his hand punching a garbage can in the dugout after a strikeout. Season over.

Frustrated with their young prospect, the Pirates left Bautista exposed for the annual Rule 5 draft that December and the Baltimore Orioles selected him, meaning they'd have to keep him in the majors to open the 2004 season or offer him back to Pittsburgh. He broke camp with the O's, collected a single off Boston's Ramiro Mendoza in his first big-league plate appearance (as a pinch-hitter), but became frustrated as the Orioles gave him just 12 appearances in the club's first 33 games. On May 25 Bautista was designated for assignment. On June 3 he was claimed off waivers by the Tampa Bay Devil Rays, as they were known then, and they gave him 15 trips to the plate in 16 games before selling him to the Kansas City Royals. His tenure there didn't last much longer, as they gave him 26 plate appearances in 29 days before trading him to the New York Mets for Justin Huber. The Mets immediately flipped Bautista back to the Pirates with Ty Wigginton and Matt Peterson for Kris Benson and Jeff Keppinger. If ever a stretch reminded a player how much of a commodity he is in the business of professional baseball, this was it. Bautista was back where he started, and all he had to show for his odyssey through transaction-wire madness were 53 plate appearances and four months of lost development time.

At least the Pirates kept him in the majors for the rest of the season, but they gave him just 43 plate appearances. For a player who hadn't risen above A-ball before and had lost half the previous season to a broken hand, the year was pretty much a writeoff. Bautista spent 2005 rebuilding his game in the minors between Double-A Altoona and Triple-A Indianapolis, enjoyed a short stint with the Pirates at season's end, and then opened 2006 back at Indy before sticking with the Pirates in early May. He posted an OPS of .755 in 117 games as a rookie with 16 home runs, and delivered similar numbers over 142 contests in 2007. But in 2008 his performance tailed off and the Pirates began to view him as a part-time player. When he was sent back to Triple-A on August 11, Bautista asked GM Neal Huntington to trade him if he could, since it seemed their relationship had run its course. Huntington placed him on revocable waivers and when Alex Anthopoulos, then a Blue Jays assistant GM, saw Bautista's name pop up, he immediately asked J.P. Ricciardi if he could put in a claim. Having traded Scott Rolen to the Cincinnati Reds a couple of weeks earlier — a deal in which Edwin Encarnacion was foisted upon them as the price to get pitching prospects Zach Stewart and Josh Roenicke — the Blue Jays needed depth at third. Bautista was a fit. Ricciardi gave the claim his blessing, Anthopoulos sent minor-league catcher Robinzon Diaz to Pittsburgh in exchange, and Bautista received a new lease on life.

During spring training that season, Bautista had drawn the attention of Anthopoulos with his big-power displays during Pirates batting practice before exhibition games. Early in June, when manager Cito Gaston replaced John Gibbons, the Blue Jays were in Pittsburgh and the slugger's bat again turned heads. Gaston and Dwayne Murphy, the new first-base coach who would eventually become hitting coach, were intrigued by Bautista's potential at age 27 but concerned about the mechanics of his swing. Huge proponents of pulling the ball, they didn't like his tendency to go the other way and started stressing the importance of starting his swing earlier. "To me it just seemed like he was wanting to go opposite field all the time, and he was always late," Murphy says. "Anything middle in, he got jammed up. He couldn't pull the ball. Everybody was busting him in, everybody knew how to pitch him." Facing batting-practice pitches, Bautista put on a show. But during games, with the pitches coming hard and in on his hands, he was lost. Says Murphy, "That's when we started talking about getting ready. 'You're so late, you've got to use both sides of the field, not just one.' That's where it really started."

The concept made sense to Bautista, but he struggled to put it into practice. Early in the 2009 season, during a conversation in the Rogers Centre weight room, Murphy stood Bautista in front of a mirror and demonstrated exactly what he was doing wrong, and how to fix the swing. It involved synchronizing the start of his high leg kick with the start of the pitcher's delivery. "He knew it wasn't right, he knew he needed that little something," says Murphy. "We sat there for a while and talked about it. The first time I remember stopping and talking to him was at the mirror in the weight room, and I just showed him what his shoulders do, and what they should do, why he didn't pull the ball, why he was so late. That leg kick, by the time the leg gets down the ball is on top of him. Then he started working on it in the cage and BP."

Bautista's sporadic playing time made it difficult to implement the changes. But on August 10, a spot opened up in right field when the Chicago White Sox claimed Alex Rios off waivers (the Blue Jays let him go, happy to be rid of the contract). With regular action, Bautista stopped fretting about when his next game would be and applied his work in the batting cage with Murphy during games more regularly. "Changes don't work with guys that don't play every day, because when they do play and they fail, they revert right back to what they were always doing," Murphy says. "They know the only way they can play is to succeed. But what he saw was the ball just jumping off his bat. Jose's a smart player, he gets it, and it seemed like he got it that fast, because he put up some good numbers that month of September."

In 27 games from September 5 to October 4, Bautista hit 10 homers, four doubles, and two triples with 21 RBIs — stats you can dream on. Yet September numbers can often be fool's gold, accomplished against some pitchers eager to go to home and others simply trying to make an impression for next year. In Bautista's case, the gold was pure. After a big spring training and a cool April in 2010, Bautista went off with 12 homers in May and hasn't stopped going deep since. He finished that season with a club record 54 homers and agreed to a $65 million, five-year extension the following spring, avoiding an arbitration hearing by mere minutes. Anthopoulos would later say no player in the history of the game has made more money off one good season, and he's right. But Bautista has lived up to it, save for the wrist injury that cost him half of 2012 and the deep bone bruise on his femur that shut him down late in 2013.

Over the span of his transformation, the Jays traded Vernon Wells and Roy Halladay, leaving a leadership void that naturally fell on Bautista to fill as the club's big bat. It's a role he's grown into. "A lot of times, if you haven't been leading on a club for a while, it's tough," says Murphy, who retired after the 2013 season. "I think it's been tough for Jose because he wants to be that guy, he wants to be the guy that leads the team, and to me he's gotten way better at it. When he first started doing it I felt he was doing some things the wrong way in trying to lead, but he was trying. I think he's gotten a lot better at it."

The mistakes arise from the double-edged sword of Bautista's emotions, Murphy says. "We've had this conversation 100 times. Sometimes it takes him out of his at-bat because he's so worried about that one pitch, but he may have one or two more. Sometimes I think it affects some at-bats and he loses the battle. He knows it, we've talked about it, he says [he's] got to stop doing it, but then the next at-bat it happens again. He's just so emotionally in the game, he wants to win, he wants to do well, but if he can ever harness that . . .

"You've also got the problem of pissing umpires off and through the course of the year, maybe not all the umpires, but there's always going to be a handful that are going to stick it on him. That's the other side of trying to convince Jose why he shouldn't do that. You can send a message to the umpire and there are a lot of guys of his calibre who do it, but they do it in a way where they don't show the umpire up." Murphy wasn't the only person who tried to hammer the point home. Manager John Gibbons, Jose Reyes, and Edwin Encarnacion all were on Bautista's case at various points of the season, too.

AS APRIL GAVE WAY to May in 2013, Bautista became much better at keeping himself under control. But on June 9, with the Jays down 6-4 to Texas and the tying runs on base, he blew up at plate umpire Gary Darling following a called first strike from closer Joe Nathan, was charged a swing on appeal for strike two, and waved at a ball in the dirt for strike three. On his way back to the dugout Bautista resumed yelling at Darling, leading to his first ejection of the season. The Jays lost 6-4. A similar scene played out July 28 against the Houston Astros, when he took two questionable strikes called by Sam Holbrook, swung through strike three, barked at the umpire, and was sent to the showers. Colby Rasmus picked Bautista up that time, delivering a walk-off RBI single in the ninth for a 2-1 win. "I think a lot of umpires misunderstand the fact that sometimes you react and you get upset and they take it personal and they shouldn't," says Bautista. "It's not necessarily that you don't like them or you hate them, it's just you get surprised when something you think is supposed to go a certain way, doesn't . . . I'm not doing it to show anybody up, I'm not doing it to make anybody look bad, I'm not doing it because I don't like those guys. I'm sure 99 percent of those guys are great guys. I don't have anything against them, I just react sometimes. Just because I do, I don't think that should affect the next call. And I believe it does, not 100 percent of the time, but a lot of times. Is it fair, unfair? I don't know. Some people say no matter what, I'm unprofessional and should be keeping my composure, and I can argue that with my way of thinking. And there are others that say it shouldn't matter and it should be objective. It's dependent on what school of thought you have on umpiring."

Through it all, Bautista says he hasn't changed his approach to umpires. Some players make small talk with them to curry favour, others trade good-natured barbs, others get creative. Former Blue Jays right-fielder Jesse Barfield, for instance, once offered Durwood Merrill a hand up as the umpire was tying a shoe, only instead of lifting him, he slipped the big wrestling fan into a half nelson instead. "The crowd went crazy, and Durwood was laughing so hard," recalled Barfield. "I got some [favourable] calls after that. It was great." Not Bautista. He's straightforward, businesslike, offering polite greetings and cordial interactions, nothing else. He's there to work, and for better or worse, the fire within is red-hot once he digs into the box. "It's been a challenge and it's been difficult, and at times I've been great at it, but at times I struggle with it," Bautista says of reining in his emotions. "I guess that's just one of my weaknesses."

Bautista batted .337 with a .742 OPS, five homers, and 16 RBIs for the month, helping the Blue Jays steady themselves from April's disastrous opening with a 13-15 record in May. A 10-6 run from May 11–29 suggested the team might have turned the corner, and was finally beginning to hit its stride. At the calendar's turn to June, the best the 2013 Blue Jays had to offer was still to come. But in a season doomed to failure, the weaknesses of both the team and its biggest star would surface again.

THE NATURAL: MARK BUEHRLE

FOLKS STOPPED AND STARED when two-year-old Mark Buehrle wound up and threw things. His parents would take him to school carnivals near their home in St. Charles, Missouri, where kids lined up to toss beanbags into the gaping mouth of a poster-board clown. Three strikes won a prize, and folks watched in amazement as the little left-hander loaded up with loot. "I don't remember it," he says, "but my parents said people were in awe of watching me."

His parents remember. John and Pat Buehrle were often asked to put a stop to it.

"Mark would wind up like he was pitching a baseball and he would nail it," John recalls. "He would miss once in a while, but more often than not, it was just one, two, three. A lot of people would come around and watch this little two-year-old pipsqueak chucking these beanbags and winning all these toys. We were asked just about every time, 'Leave. Let somebody else win.'"

Mark Buehrle has a gift. To this day, if you ask him how he has made millions by throwing balls and hitting targets, he will say he has no clue. "It just kind of came naturally," he says. "I just threw the ball where it had to go and it went there. I've always been that way."

By the time he became a Blue Jay, Buehrle had developed one of the most respected reputations in baseball, and perhaps the most unusual. Among starting pitchers in this century, he is the most durable, having spent nary a day on the disabled list. Year after year, he has been utterly consistent, averaging 200-plus innings and 14 victories, deriving his success from inviting batters to hit his pitches. He is the fastest worker and the best fielder. His fastball is one of the slowest. And his accuracy, from the beanbag-toss to the big leagues, has remained remarkable.

ENTERING 2013, NO PITCHER had logged more innings during the period Buehrle was a starter (2001–2012). Over the dozen years before coming to Toronto, he averaged 6.7 innings per start. No pitcher had allowed more hits either, yet Buehrle beseeches batters to hit his pitches, preferring ordinary outs to strikeouts. And he has always owned the strike zone. Over his career, he has averaged two walks per nine innings. Remarkably, he has never missed a start.

In the glow of the Jays' off-season, when discouraging words were seldom heard, someone would occasionally raise two essential questions about the 34-year-old Buehrle: How long can he keep doing what he has done so well for so long? How would he fare in the tough American League East, where his career ERA was a shade over 5.00?

By early May, when his ERA was 7.02, and he was leading the league in runs and home runs allowed, and he had already lost twice to the Yankees and once to the Red Sox, those questions had risen from whispers to growls.

But then, on May 11, with the Jays already 11 games below .500, Buehrle faced the Red Sox in Fenway Park and delivered an early-season elixir. He shut out Boston over seven innings, leaving after a leadoff walk in the eighth that eventually scored. The Jays won 3-2.

From that day through June 23, the team went 24-12. In the same period, Buehrle posted a 2.65 ERA and yielded only two homers in 51 innings. "I think he springboarded us," said pitching coach Pete Walker.

FROM LITTLE LEAGUE INTO his teens, Buehrle was a scrawny pitching-prodigy in summer leagues. Yet when he tried out for his high school's freshman and sophomore teams in grades nine and 10, he was cut both times.

"He was dejected," his father says. "He couldn't believe it. We never really could get a direct answer from the coach. I didn't want to force myself on a coach and say, 'Why aren't you taking my son?' I was sure he got enough of that. I assumed there was a decent reason."

The next year, in grade 11, Mark was loath to risk rejection again. When his dad asked him about the tryout dates for the varsity team, he was evasive. Finally, his dad called the coach. Tryouts had been running for almost two weeks. The last one was the next afternoon.

That evening after dinner, Mark was doing homework in his bedroom when his father walked in. "I told him I called the coach and found out about the tryouts," John says. "He just gave me that deer-in-the-headlights look."

As Mark faced his father in his room that night in 1996, he talked about the hurt he still felt from failing twice to make the team. He did not throw hard, and he was small for his age those first two years, but he had been a standout pitcher in summer leagues, chosen annually to play on travel teams. He could not understand why Francis Howell North High School could not find a roster spot for him. Twice bitten, he did not want to take a third strike.

His dad said Mark would have to make his own choice. But John Buehrle, a big, soft-spoken man, also had a stern message for his son.

"I said, 'You're going to go through life and you're going to have times when you're going to get knocked on your butt, times when you get turned down or rejected. That's all part of life. You've got to take the negatives and try to find something positive. You can't quit. Your mother and I, we didn't raise quitters. If you quit now, you'll never make it. You'll quit the rest of your life. It's up to you.' Then I told him it was his decision. I had no clue what he was going to do."

Anxious to find out what Mark decided, his dad came home early the next day from his job as the city's water systems manager. Mark, who usually got home at 3 p.m., wheeled his car into the driveway at nearly six o'clock and entered the house wearing a poker face.

"Then he just busted out this big ol' smile from ear to ear," John recalls. "He said, 'Dad, I made it.' We gave each other a big hug, and cried. We had a real good time that night . . .

"If I hadn't talked to him the night before, I honestly think Mark would be flipping burgers or selling cars. Nothing wrong with those careers, but I don't think he'd be in baseball today."

JUNE STARTED SLOWLY for the Jays, but their pitching picture brightened. In the first six games, the staff allowed just over two runs per game. A couple of clunkers followed, and then came the streak: 11 consecutive wins, in which the team morphed from jalopy to Lamborghini. Superb pitching, clutch contributions from everyone in the lineup, and a run of luck combined to transform Toronto into baseball's best team.

Briefly.

Buehrle, R.A. Dickey, Josh Johnson, and converted reliever Esmil Rogers each enjoyed their best months to date. Chien-Ming Wang, signed off the scrap heap, helped ignite the streak and flamed out when it ended, his improbable success one of several signs that the streak was like a comet flashing across the dark sky of the Jays' dismal season.

But unlike some of his teammates, Buehrle was no comet. His June record was only 2-2, but he kept the team within striking distance in each of his six starts. He was pitching in the manner to which he, and his teammates from previous years, had become accustomed: efficient but unspectacular, consistently giving the Jays a chance to win.

BUEHRLE CAN'T REMEMBER A time when he didn't have a glove on one hand and a ball in the other. When he started playing Little League ball in St. Charles, his favourite position was catcher. But Little League is the last bastion for left-handed catchers, and Buehrle was born to throw strikes — so he pitched, and he was a natural.

"I think I matured late," he says. "I remember seeing my high school ID card from my junior year. You could tell from my face how small I was. I've always been a pinpoint-control guy, but when I got to college and matured, and started working out and doing cardio and getting on weight programs, the velocity kind of came with it."

After finally making his high school team, he excelled, drawing interest from 11 colleges, including such prominent baseball schools as Louisiana State and Oklahoma State. But he and his family felt he would have a better chance to play regularly at a small school. They chose Jefferson College, close to home in south St. Louis, thanks in part to a friendship between Bob Dunahue, his high school coach, and Dave Oster, Jefferson's coach.

Oster also was a part-time scout for the White Sox. On Oster's recommendation, they sent several scouts to watch Buehrle, then drafted him, inauspiciously, in the 38th round after his first year at Jefferson. He was the 1,139th player chosen. Most players drafted that late languish for two or three years in the minors, never to be heard from again.

Buehrle chose to pitch another college season and finish his two-year criminal justice program before signing. On the day after he graduated in May 1999, he left home to join Chicago's Class A team in Burlington, Iowa.

He was 20. It took him less than two years to reach the major leagues.

THE BLUE JAYS' STREAK started in Chicago with a dramatic 10-inning win, triggered by Jose Bautista's game-tying homer in the ninth inning. But as the Blue Jays pulled into Texas for a four-game series, logic suggested they would be fortunate to win a game or two. They had never swept a four-game series in Arlington. Their record there was 81-115. And the Rangers were 13 games over .500 as they battled Oakland for the American League West lead.

Four wins later, the Jays had outscored the Rangers 24-2. Rogers, Buehrle, Dickey, and Wang each worked deep into their starts and earned a win. Colby Rasmus had only three hits in the whole series, but all were home runs and were good for six RBIs. Only the first game was close.

Buehrle's start was his best of the season to date. In an 8-0 win, he pitched seven innings, gave up four hits and a walk, and struck out seven. Aided by two ground-ball double plays, he faced only three batters over the minimum.

THE TRADE THAT BROUGHT Buehrle and four other Miami Marlins to Toronto not only stunned and embittered the veteran left-hander,

but also complicated his family life and triggered a small political con-
tretemps in Ontario. After spending the first 12 years of his pro career
with the Chicago White Sox, Buehrle had signed a four-year, $54 mil-
lion free-agent contract with Miami before the 2012 season. Suddenly,
less than a year later, a man accustomed to staying in one place was on
the move again, not only to a different country but also to a jurisdic-
tion that had outlawed one of his beloved family pets. While Blue Jays
fans rejoiced, Buehrle fumed.

In an angry statement issued through his agent three days after the
trade, Buehrle said the Marlins had given him "repeated assurances"
that they were committed to keeping him for the duration of his contract. "I was lied to on multiple occasions," he said. In keeping with
club policy, the Marlins did not give Buehrle a no-trade clause, but
he said owner Jeffrey Loria had pledged to keep him in the fold as the
Marlins, buoyed by a bevy of high-priced stars and a new stadium,
entered what they advertised as the start of a golden era. By the end of
July, they were 14 games out of first place and had begun to off-load
their best players to other teams.

Still stinging from what he considered a profound betrayal by
Miami, Buehrle was stung again by the Ontario law banning the breed
of dogs generally known as pit bulls. A year and a half earlier, during
Buehrle's final season with the White Sox, his wife, Jamie, had rescued
a Staffordshire terrier from euthanasia at a Chicago-area facility. They
named him Slater. Like their three other dogs, all Vizslas, Slater became
a cherished member of the Buehrle family, adored by Mark, Jamie,
their son, Braden, six, and daughter, Brooklyn, four.

Staffordshire terriers are among the pit bull types banned in
Ontario since 2005. Passed in the wake of several vicious dog attacks,
the Ontario statute is similar to a local law in Miami-Dade County,
where the Buehrles sought to settle a year earlier. They solved that
problem by buying a house in a suburb while Jamie, an ardent pet-
adoption activist, helped lead the opposition to the bylaw.

But this time, Niagara Falls, N.Y., was the city closest to Toronto
where Slater would be welcome. The commute was not appealing,
nor was the prospect of leaving Slater in someone else's care for the
summer. So the Buehrles eventually decided that Mark would live

alone in Toronto while his family stayed at home in St. Louis, making occasional visits during the season.

Meanwhile, without even living in Ontario, Mark and Jamie had become the most prominent critics of the province's "breed-specific" legislation. So in Buehrle's introductory conference call with Toronto reporters, Slater dominated the narrative. If a dog turns bad, Buehrle said, hold the owner responsible, not the animal. "It's a discriminatory law," he said. "Just because of the way a dog looks, I don't think that dog should be banned."

For a player the Jays acquired to help them win a championship, it was a bizarre and strained welcome.

FORTUNATELY, THE STRAIN WAS not apparent when spring training opened. Within a few days after the players reported to Dunedin, it became clear that Buehrle was upbeat and accessible. As awkward as his transition from Miami to Toronto had been, he seemed at home as he settled into the corner of the clubhouse that also included Darren Oliver, Josh Johnson, and R.A. Dickey, and he made fast friends with his teammates, beginning a good-natured exchange with Ricky Romero about their respective walk totals.

Buehrle is friendly, witty, and family-oriented, an unpretentious veteran with a ready smile and a zealous competitive streak. He says he does not deliberately take on a leadership role, but it seems to come naturally, much like his accomplishments on the pitcher's mound.

He is indeed a natural. The art and science of his craft converged early and organically, spawning an effortless delivery that appears lifted from a textbook. It took diligence, of course, but for a kid with a gift, that was the fun part. "Every day I wanted to practise," he says. "I wanted to be out on a field doing something, or have Mom and Dad in the backyard, playing catch with [me] non-stop."

For most who find success at the professional level, pitching demands systematic adjustments in body mechanics — the arm angle, the torso twist, the stride span — until something finally clicks. Buehrle was born with all of that. His delivery is fluid and uncomplicated, his control uncanny. Coaches helped him with the basics and showed him how to throw various pitches, but not much has changed since Little

League, except that the skinny kid blossomed into a 6-foot-2, 244-pound pitching machine.

BUT UNLIKE THE KID at the school carnival, the grown-up Buehrle tends to blend into the crowd. Yes, he has enjoyed shining moments — two no-hitters (one a perfect game) and a World Series championship with the White Sox — along with a reputation for durability, consistency, and agility. But over the course of a season, Buehrle does not hog the highlight reel. He is a blue-collar worker, getting the job done by persuading batters to hit what he throws, tantalizing them with pinpoint control at the edges of the strike zone and a fastball which, by big-league standards, is not fast at all.

"I don't throw hard," he says, "so I'm less injury prone. There are days you go out there, you don't feel the greatest, but you do what you have to do." And he does it with distinctly unspectacular tools, while following a routine that some baseball insiders might consider heresy: he rarely throws in the bullpen between starts, and ignores scouting reports on his opponents.

"I'm not a big video guy," he says. "I don't study film. I don't throw many bullpens; it's less wear and tear. I'll throw one once in a while if I really need to work on a pitch. But mainly I just pitch, and in between starts, I play catch."

Advance scouts assemble meticulous reports on opponents, but Buehrle prefers to rely on his catcher. At 34, he is an elder statesman, so most catchers would happily defer to his judgement if he shook off a sign. But he chooses to work without complications. Get the sign. See the target. Throw the ball. Whatever happens, don't second-guess the previous pitch.

And ignore the radar gun. The average major-league fastball registers between 90 and 91 miles per hour, but upon entering the 2013 season, after 12 years as a big-league starter, Buehrle had averaged about 86, according to Fangraphs.com. Only seven regular starters during that period threw slower fastballs. Two of them were knuckleballers: R.A. Dickey, Buehrle's new teammate with the Blue Jays, and Tim Wakefield, one of Dickey's mentors.

Buehrle had kept batters off balance throughout his career by complementing his fastball with a curveball and changeup. He may top out at 86, but he averages 72 with his curveball and 79 with his changeup, and he compounds the challenge for a hitter because he uses so little time between pitches. Over his career, he has averaged 16.7 seconds between pitches, the fastest pace in the majors. (He once pitched a complete game that took one hour and 39 minutes.)

Adam Lind first faced Buehrle in 2007. Buehrle handcuffed him with inside fastballs. They did not meet again for a year, but Lind remembered. "So I was ready for the heaters inside, even stepping in the bucket a little bit trying to cheat, and this time, it was all slow — really slow — curveballs away." Four months later, they met again. Buehrle struck out Lind three times. "You're ready for the slow stuff," Lind said, "but he seems like he can always throw a little slower."

Mark DeRosa managed six hits in 25 career at-bats against Buehrle before they became teammates in 2013. He likens Buehrle to the great Tom Glavine, another soft-tossing southpaw control-artist whom DeRosa came to know when they were fellow Atlanta Braves in the early 2000s.

"It's always a stressful at-bat against Buehrle because he works so quick," DeRosa says. "He knows how to pitch, works the ball in and out, adds and subtracts [velocity] on everything he throws, works super fast. He gets it and goes. He makes you uncomfortable."

AS THE BRIEF EUPHORIA of June faded and the Jays settled back into the sediment, Buehrle kept doing what he has done since the White Sox drafted him in 1998: serving up slow pitches at a fast pace, painting the edges of the strike zone, coaxing ground balls, and claiming fate helps him when he wins and hurts him when he loses. "I got away with a lot of mistakes tonight," he often says after a good game. Looking back at a loss, he frequently cites the ground balls that slip past diving defenders or a good pitch that an opponent hit into the seats.

"I think you make your own luck," says pitching coach Pete Walker. "I've heard him mention luck, too, but I don't think he's pitched 12 years consecutively, making all those starts, due to luck. It's hard work, it's a great frame of mind, it's understanding who he is as a pitcher and what he needs to do. He never tries to do too much. I think that's what the other pitchers see in him. He doesn't try to make his curveball nasty, or make his changeup nasty. He just stays within himself and pitches."

And win or lose, he is a study in equilibrium. Walker says Buehrle's work ethic is constant and scholarly. In the early season, as his ERA soared past 7.00, he spent extra time trying to fix his changeup. He occasionally mentioned his frustration to Walker, but never let it drag him down, nor let it show around his teammates.

Josh Johnson, who was a Buehrle teammate in 2012 before they both were traded to Toronto, marvels at Buehrle's ability to remain both resolute and upbeat, whether he gives up no runs or seven runs (he did both in 2013).

"He's always a good time in the dugout," Johnson says. "Even when he's pitching, he's always talking and joking around — maybe even more when he's pitching. He makes you realize that it's still a game and you need to have fun."

Johnson tends to brood over his own struggles — he had much to brood about in 2013 — but he smiles quickly when asked whether he has ever seen Buehrle display frustration.

"I don't think I've ever seen him frustrated at all, at anything, unless it's something about hunting and how he can't hunt 24/7 all year long," Johnson said.

In his first year as a big-league pitching coach, Walker had to dig deep to deal with a struggling staff, from Ricky Romero's dispiriting descent to Dickey's search for his Cy Young groove to Johnson's sagging confidence as he endured one stressful start after another. All the while, Buehrle was the rock, Walker says.

"He brings a sense of calmness to the staff and to his teammates when he's out there," he said. "I think they can learn from that."

BUEHRLE CANNOT EXPLAIN HOW he has stayed so calm for so long under the major-league microscope. Genetics probably has something to do with it. But he will say this: early in his career, he learned to erase the previous pitch from his memory. For many pitchers, it is the hardest part of the job. Many in the fraternity ask him how he does it.

"They say they throw a pitch and a guy hits a home run, that's all they're thinking of. Yeah, it does suck, and I don't want to give up a home run or a walk, but at the same time you can't do anything about it. If you're thinking about what just happened on that pitch, the next pitch you're going to screw up even more and then you're going to get yourself into even more trouble and that opens the floodgates . . . The younger you are, the harder it is to let it go.

"But I've always taken pride in doing that. Yeah, after a game, I can be frustrated and upset, but at the same time you won't be able to tell because I try to be the same guy, whether I win the start or I get my ass handed to me. That next day and the days before the next start, I try to stay even keel. You do your work. You have fun. There's no reason when you're winning to be too high or when you're losing to be too low."

That may be the most important lesson pitching colleagues can learn from Buehrle. They certainly do not envy his fastball velocity or the number of hits he gives up, and they're unlikely to buck baseball tradition and start skipping bullpen sessions between starts. But players respect success and look to veterans for cues.

Fellow pitchers who seek Buehrle's advice receive a simple answer. *Do your work. Have fun. Don't walk people. Forget about the last pitch.*

Just don't ask him how he does it. "I can't watch a guy pitch and say, 'Your arm's dropping, or you're doing this or that,'" he says. "I can't see that. People ask me how I throw something. I say, 'I hold the ball here.' Then what? 'I don't know. I throw it.' It's hard to explain."

AFTER BUEHRLE WENT ON to stardom in the big leagues, his high school coach was often asked why Mark was cut twice. Bob Dunahue, still the only head coach Francis Howell North High School has ever had, says he had seen Mark in the sophomore (grade 10) tryouts and told the coach in charge of the team to keep him on the roster. Dunahue says the assistant coach later claimed he omitted Mark's name by mistake when he posted the final list.

"I ended up firing that coach," Dunahue says.

Sometime after Mark made the varsity team, Dunahue instituted a new policy. All cuts from the freshman, sophomore, and varsity tryouts would require his approval. Dunahue called it The Buehrle Rule.

Dunahue says he had been impressed when he saw Mark dominate a tough opponent in a game the previous summer. Another strong impression: Mark had grown from 5-foot-4 as a freshman to 6-foot-1 as a junior. The day after John and Mark Buehrle chatted in Mark's room, Dunahue says he sought out Mark in the school cafeteria and told him he did not need to try out; he had a spot on the varsity team.

Buehrle smiles at the story. He does not remember Dunahue approaching him in the cafeteria. "I'm not saying he didn't, but I don't recall any of that," he says. Dunahue also gives the impression that he and Mark remain in regular contact: he says they exchanged texts after several of Buehrle's major-league milestones. Buehrle smiles again. "I haven't talked to him probably since high school," he says.

He is certain of one thing.

"Dad told me that he and Mom didn't raise quitters. That was the reason I went back out for the team."

JUNE DID NOT END well for the Jays. Their record for the month was 17-9, but they lost five of seven after the streak. Buehrle started the last game of June, a 5-4 loss in Fenway Park that in many ways epitomized their season.

During his six innings, Buehrle gave up four runs. The Jays scored two while squandering several promising opportunities. Then they scored a third, and in the top of the ninth, Bautista hit a homer to tie the score, just as he had in Chicago on the night the streak began.

But this time, substitute first baseman Josh Thole — playing only because Lind had to leave with back spasms — made an error that handed Boston a walk-off win.

At the precise halfway point of their season, the Blue Jays were 40-41, eight and a half games behind the first-place Red Sox and six games behind in the wild-card sweepstakes.

"That may be the most frustrating loss of the year, to be honest with you, simply because of who we're playing, where we're at, and so many opportunities," Gibbons said. "I can't remember that many opportunities we let get away."

Soon, he would remember more.

10 | THE STREAK

AFTER TANTALIZING THEIR FANS in December and deflating them in April, the Blue Jays turned on the tease again in June. Before they sashayed out of the shadows, they gave no hint they were about to become the hottest team in baseball. But suddenly, they shed all of their failures — the shoddy work by the starters, the inability to grab an early lead, the utter ineptitude of the offence with runners in scoring position.

They won 11 in a row, matching a club record accomplished twice previously.

Hope returned. The Jays started the streak with a 27-36 record. Eleven games later, they had pushed past the .500 mark for the first time all season, slipped out of last place, and climbed to within three games of the wild-card lead. The rotation entered the streak with a collective ERA of 5.31. For the next 11 games, it was 2.76. For the season, Jays batters had hit .244 with runners in scoring position; over the streak, they batted .343. In their first 63 games, the Jays scored first 29 times. In the 11-game streak, they scored first 10 times.

And the bullpen, the team's forte all season, continued to shine. The relievers allowed only two earned runs during the streak and logged an ERA of 0.63.

This was the stuff of dreams when fans surveyed the revamped roster back in December, the sort of consistency the baseball literati projected when the season opened. Fuelling further optimism was the imminent return of shortstop Jose Reyes, who was living up to his credentials as the team's best all-around player before he wrecked his ankle on an ill-advised slide while playing in just his 10th game as a Blue Jay.

"I fully expect us to continue to play this way," veteran Mark DeRosa said. "I think Jose Reyes is going to be a huge shot of adrenaline for us. That's not a knock against anybody he will replace, but he's one of the best players in the game. How can he not be just a huge bolt of energy for this lineup?"

The man Reyes would replace was Munenori Kawasaki, whose overachievement during the streak was typical of his team. Kawasaki was batting .216 when the surge started. Over the next 11 games, he batted .292 with a double, two triples, and — wonder of wonders — the first home run of his career, which triggered a come-from-behind win against Baltimore in the ninth game.

During the streak, Colby Rasmus batted .148, but four of his hits were homers. Maicer Izturis drove in seven runs; he had driven in six over the previous two months. Jose Bautista batted .163, but hit two homers — the first to send Game 1 into extra innings, the other to win Game 10. J.P. Arencibia had three homers and seven RBIs in June; all of his homers and all but one of his RBIs came during the streak.

Throughout the streak and the month, the steady hitting of Adam Lind and Edwin Encarnacion carried the offence. Lind hit .350 for June with seven homers and 22 RBIs while Encarnacion batted .277 with eight homers and 20 RBIs. Each had four homers and 12 RBIs during the streak. It was one of the rare periods during the season when Lind and Encarnacion enjoyed strong, consistent support from others in the lineup.

Besides Kawasaki, perhaps no one epitomized the June aberration more than Chien-Ming Wang, an over-the-hill pitcher who was signed in desperation to fill the revolving fifth starter's job. After he won 19 games for the Yankees in 2006 and again in 2007, a series of injuries drove Wang from the majors and he started the 2013 season as a Triple-A guest of the Yankees. He made six starts for the Jays, the first three during the streak. In those three, he compiled a 2.61 ERA. In his next two starts, he failed to survive the second inning, prompting the Jays to ship him to Buffalo.

The streak started in Chicago against the White Sox, a last-place club, and continued in Texas against a good Rangers team in a down cycle (they had lost seven of 11 before dropping four to Toronto). Then the Jays came home to play a mediocre Colorado club that had just lost its best player, Troy Tulowitzki, to injury. The toughest opponent of the streak came last: Baltimore had won eight of its previous 11 games and was nudging Boston for first place in the American League East. The Jays beat the Orioles in two close games and a laugher.

So for those who cared to look, there were plenty of signs that the Jays' 17-9 record in June was unsustainable, fuelled as it was by a streak featuring atypical individual and team performances. But for many in the fan base — and many players as well — who entered the season with lofty expectations, the 11-game run renewed belief that a long, gloomy night was over. The team was simply starting to fulfill its destiny. It would be a daunting challenge, but the inevitable playoff run was at hand, made more exciting by the late start.

"The pieces are there for us to stay hot for an extended period of time," DeRosa said. "How hot we get and how hot we stay remains to be seen, but I wouldn't count us out."

When the surge ended, in a 4-1 home loss to Tampa Bay, Gibbons praised his team for playing consistently solid baseball at last, and expressed confidence that the winning would continue.

"It's been a nice little streak," the manager said. "Start another one tomorrow."

The Blue Jays responded by losing eight of their next 11 games, allowing 57 runs in the process. They were back to normal.

1.

Tuesday, June 11, U.S. Cellular Field, Chicago
BLUE JAYS 7, WHITE SOX 5 (10 innings)

Toronto was down to its last strike when Jose Bautista tied the score at 5-5 with a home run off White Sox closer Addison Reed. In the 10th, Rajai Davis singled, stole second, moved up on a fly ball, and scored on a wild pitch. Maicer Izturis singled and scored after a Munenori Kawasaki double, when the catcher failed to handle the throw from the outfield. In his Blue Jays debut, Chien-Ming Wang gave up five runs in 7 1/3 innings.

```
Toronto   020   020   001   2     7  13  0
CWS       010   400   000   0     5  11  3
```
W: Cecil (2-0). L: Troncoso (0-1). SV: Janssen (13).
HR – Tor: Encarnacion (18), Bautista (15). CWS: Dunn (17), Gillaspie (4).

2.
Thursday, June 13, Rangers Ballpark, Arlington
BLUE JAYS 3, RANGERS 1

In his third start after opening the season as a reliever, Esmil Rogers battled Texas ace Yu Darvish to a 1-1 tie through seven innngs. After a throwing error by four-time Gold Glove third baseman Adrian Beltre opened the eighth, Edwin Encarnacion's two-out, two-run double put Toronto ahead to stay.

```
Toronto   001   000   020   3   4   0
Texas     010   000   000   1   6   1
```
W: Rogers (2-2). L: Cotts (2-1). SV: Janssen (14).
HR – Tor: none. Texas. Cruz (16).

3.
Friday, June 14, Rangers Ballpark, Arlington
BLUE JAYS 8, RANGERS 0

Colby Rasmus hit a three-run homer and J.P. Arencibia a solo shot, both in the fourth inning, and the Jays cruised behind Mark Buehrle, who allowed four hits and struck out seven in seven innings.

```
Toronto   000   410   111   8   11   0
Texas     000   000   000   0    5   0
```
W: Buehrle (3-4). L: Grimm (5-5).
HR – Tor: Rasmus (11), Arencibia (13). Texas: none.

4.

Saturday, June 15, Rangers Ballpark, Arlington
BLUE JAYS 6, RANGERS 1

The Jays did it again with homers. Adam Lind hit a two-run shot in the first and Rasmus made it two in two days with a two-run blast in the fourth. R.A. Dickey held Texas to one run over 5 2/3 innings.

Toronto	200	200	002	6	8	0
Texas	000	001	000	1	9	1

W: Dickey (6-8). L: Lindblom (0-2).
HR – Tor: Lind (7), Rasmus (12). Texas: none.

5.

Sunday, June 16, Rangers Ballpark, Arlington
BLUE JAYS 7, RANGERS 2

On the advice of his coaches, Wang began complementing his trademark sinker with off-speed pitches and blanked Texas over seven innings. Toronto maintained its long-ball surge: Lind hit a three-run homer, Arencibia a two-run blast, and Rasmus a solo shot. Lind had seven hits and drove in six runs in the four-game series.

Toronto	020	100	400	7	12	1
Texas	000	000	002	2	8	0

WP: Wang (1-0). LP: Holland (5-4).
HR – Tor: Arencibia (14), Rasmus (13), Lind (8). Texas: none.

6.

Monday, June 17, Rogers Centre, Toronto
BLUE JAYS 2, ROCKIES 0

Toronto's Josh Johnson and Colorado's Jorge De La Rosa battled to a scoreless draw through seven innings. In the eighth, Davis singled and stole second, Rasmus walked, and both advanced on a ground-out. Then Maicer

Izturis blooped a two-run single to left field. Brett Cecil and Casey Janssen held the score right there.

```
Colorado 000    000    000    0  5  0
Toronto  000    000    02x    2  3  0
```
WP: Cecil (3-0). LP: Belisle (4-4). SV: Janssen (15).
HR – none.

7.
Tuesday, June 18, Rogers Centre, Toronto
BLUE JAYS 8, ROCKIES 3

The Jays took a 4-0 lead in the first inning without the aid of a home run. Then Encarnacion hit a two-run blast in the fifth and Izturis and Arencibia delivered solo shots in the sixth. Rogers allowed three runs (two earned) over 6 2/3 innings.

```
Colorado 000    000    030    3  4  2
Toronto  400    022    00x    8  11 2
```
WP: Rogers (3-2). LP: Francis (2-5).
HR – Colo: none. Tor: Encarnacion (19), Izturis (4), Arencibia (15).

8.
Wednesday, June 19, Rogers Centre, Toronto
BLUE JAYS 5, ROCKIES 2

Lind's three-run homer in the first gave Toronto another early lead. Then it was Buehrle (five innings, two runs) and the bullpen for the win.

```
Colorado 010    010    000    2  9  2
Toronto  300    100    10x    5  7  1
```
WP: Buehrle (4-4). LP: Nicasio (4-3). SV: Janssen (16).
HR – Colo: C. Gonzalez (21). Tor: Lind (9).

9.

Friday, June 21, Rogers Centre, Toronto
BLUE JAYS 7, ORIOLES 6

The Jays reached the .500 mark for the first time, winning a wild one when Davis ripped a walk-off RBI single in the bottom of the ninth. Kawasaki brought more than 35,000 fans to their feet in the seventh with the first homer of his career, a two-run shot that tied the score 6-6. Dickey worked into the seventh inning, but gave up three homers and six runs.

Baltimore 010   004   100   6 7 0
Toronto   200   011   201   7 9 0
WP: Janssen (2-0). LP: Matusz (2-1).
HR – Balt: Hardy (15), Davis (27), Flaherty (3). Tor: Lind (10), Encarnacion (20), Kawasaki (1).

10.

Saturday, June 22, Rogers Centre, Toronto
BLUE JAYS 4, ORIOLES 2

The previous night, Orioles reliever Darren O'Day struck out Bautista and fired a few triumphant remarks in the slugger's direction. This time, they faced off again in the bottom of the eighth and Bautista exacted his revenge with a tie-breaking two-run homer, chirping a retort at O'Day as he rounded third base. Wang had another good start, allowing one run in 6 1/3 innings.

Baltimore 000   010   010   2 7 0
Toronto   100   010   02x   4 4 0
WP: Oliver (3-1). LP: M. Gonzalez (5-3). SV: Janssen (17).
HR – Balt: Teagarden (2). Tor: Izturis (5), Bautista (16).

11.

Sunday, June 23, Rogers Centre, Toronto
BLUE JAYS 13, ORIOLES 5

The Jays amassed nine of their 14 hits in the first three innings and took a 9-0 lead, thereby easing the drill for Josh Johnson, who allowed four runs in six innings. Encarnacion had three hits, including a two-run homer, and drove in four runs. Bautista capped the rout with a three-run double in the seventh.

Baltimore	000	002	201	5	11	0
Toronto	135	000	40x	13	14	1

WP: Johnson (1-2). LP: Garcia (3-5).
HR – Balt: Flaherty 2 (5). Tor: Encarnacion (21), Rasmus (14).

11 | "I AM JAH-PAH-NEEEEESE!"

ON THE EVENING OF June 23, after the Blue Jays had won their 11th consecutive game in a home sweep of the Baltimore Orioles, Jose Bautista tweeted an Instagram video from the team's charter flight to Tampa. The 15-second clip showed Munenori Kawasaki, *sans* suit jacket but with tie neatly in place, dancing in the aisle as teammates laughed and cheered him on in the background. As he gyrated to the music and spoke non-stop in Japanese, Kawasaki kept an eye on the camera, as if to ask, "Am I still on?"

Among teammates and fans, Kawasaki is always on. A bubbling fountain of spontaneity and fun, he seems to carry a jester gene in his DNA, as if he were born to amuse, having discovered at a young age how easily he could make people smile and generate mutual warmth and affection. "It's very rare, if you say to a person 'I like you,' that the person will not like you back,'" he says.

In a Blue Jays season so heavily stocked with misery and disappointment, it was impossible not to fall for Kawasaki, who at the most basic of levels simply made people happy. Teammates loved his frenetic energy and unbridled enthusiasm, even if they could barely understand him most of the time. In many ways their admiration for him was a unifying force in the clubhouse. Fans loved his quirky antics, endearing catchphrases, and joyful exuberance. Few had experienced anyone like him before, and with so many people looking for something positive to latch onto, the slight infielder with borderline big-league talent turned into a phenomenon.

"I think in the history of baseball there's never been a player like him, and there will never be another player like him," says Ichiro Suzuki, the typically reserved Japanese icon idolized by Kawasaki, speaking through interpreter Allen Turner. "I think the name Kawasaki should just be its own species. It should be a category by itself. That's how much different he is than [other] players I've come in contact with."

Neither the Blue Jays nor their fans knew what to expect when the club first summoned Kawasaki from Triple-A Buffalo on April 13 to fill in for injured shortstop Jose Reyes. Signed to a minor-league contract late in spring training to provide infield depth, he was unknown to most Toronto fans, unless they were paying close attention to the Seattle Mariners in 2012, when he played in the majors for the first time at age 31 and batted .192. Those who Googled his name came quickly upon a YouTube video of him doing a Michael Jackson dance turn in the Mariners dugout. It was a taste of things to come.

Early in his first game at the Rogers Centre, after Kawasaki slid into third base with a triple, he leaped to attention, faced his dugout, and solemnly saluted his teammates with his fingers in a V framing his right eye. As the game progressed, he routinely placed his hands together and bowed to his teammates on the field. He did deep knee-bends between pitches during at-bats. He cheered incessantly in the dugout, although it was all in Japanese and his teammates had no idea what he was saying.

By the eighth inning, the crowd was chanting his name. He had been a Blue Jay for three days.

For the next two and a half months, the chants continued. In a game where stoicism is mainstream and flamboyance is reserved for brief star turns, Kawasaki was an anomaly, a daily reminder that baseball, at its heart, is a kid's game that should be fun. Why not show it? He was 32, going on 12, and let's face it, were he not an impish Japanese player who often made fun of the fact that he spoke little English, the hidebound world of big-league baseball probably would have frowned at his antics. But Kawasaki's unusual blend of innocence and cunning was irresistible.

During batting practice, he slapped sharp grounders to the opposite field and worked on bunting while his teammates hit meatball pitches over the fence. Once in a great while, Kawasaki hit a batting-practice home run too, prompting shouts of "Noodles!" from his brethren. Kawasaki refers to his arms as noodles, mocking his lack of power, and when he does happen to hit a long ball, he pulls up his sleeve and stares admiringly at his flexed biceps as teammates hoot and howl.

BUT TO LOCK IN on the shtick is to gloss over the substance. Kawasaki was an eight-time all-star in Japan, where he played for the Fukuoka Softbank Hawks, and represented his country in the 2008 Olympics in Beijing and at the 2006 and 2009 editions of the World Baseball Classic. He modelled his game after Suzuki, whom he befriended at the first WBC ("He was just always there," Suzuki recalls with a smile), and accepted a minor-league contract from the Mariners before the 2012 season because he so badly wanted to play alongside his idol. Rather than return to Japan after his release last winter, Kawasaki was intent on remaining in North America despite his Seattle struggles. There is much more to him beneath the surface, yet everybody simply embraces the perpetually positive personality. "That's why I think he might have inner struggle, because of the fact that that's what people assume, that's what people expect out of him," says Suzuki. "It's great that people think that, but he's got to keep that up. Like for example, if a singer sings a sad song the way it's supposed to be sung — sad — that's what we're supposed to expect. But if you have a singer sing a sad song with happiness, with an outgoing personality, that I think is sad, listening to somebody sing a sad song that way. He must have some kind of personal struggle at times. Even though he's a special species, probably on its own, he is still human, and sometimes I wish people would [recognize] that he is human, and he's not always like that, not just one-dimensional."

Few bothered to look, too enamoured with the bowing and dancing, along with the batting-practice handstands and the cartoonish, knee-pumping bluffs toward second base. Every so often, he would deliver the unpredictable — a game-changing hit, which would generate rollicking chants and a standing ovation, and some of the most unusual and entertaining post-game interviews on record.

After his game-winning two-run double on May 26, Kawasaki was carried off the field on his teammates' shoulders. Moments later, he came to his clubhouse scrum armed with a Japanese-English phrase book. He thumbed the pages, found a suitable cliché and declared, "I did it." Then, from another page, another deadpan one-liner, "Give me a hug." And another, "It was boring." He said his big hit made him "very, very, very happy." Then he added, "I am Japanese. Next, please."

One night in Cleveland, after another game-winning hit, a reporter asked how he felt when he heard a raucous group of visiting Blue Jays fans chanting his name. "I am exciting," he replied. He might have meant to say, "I am excited." Both were accurate.

Kawasaki's choice of English quips left observers to wonder whether he understood what he was saying. No matter. This was performance art, complete with comic timing, a poker face, and a twinkling eye. But as pitcher Esmil Rogers observed a few weeks later, Kawasaki took his phrase book seriously.

"He learns Spanish and he learns English too," said Rogers, a native of the Dominican Republic. "He's a good guy, he's a smart guy. He's got a book. He says he reads his book every day and every day he comes to the stadium with something new, some word that he learned and brings it here to use."

Several Latin players bonded with Kawasaki immediately, perhaps because they could empathize as he battled the language barrier, but also because they come from a culture that celebrates the sort of vivacity that Kawasaki personifies. Rogers and Emilio Bonifacio quickly became his closest friends on the team, thereby starting a series of trilingual language lessons in the clubhouse. Within hours of Kawasaki's arrival, Bonifacio taught him the Spanish phrase "lo viste" — "see that?" — and showed him the V eye-salute that Bonifacio invented to go with it. In turn, Kawasaki taught his friends a few Japanese phrases. When Kawasaki stepped into the batter's box, he often heard Rogers shouting in Japanese from the bench, "Let's go, you can do it!"

And Kawasaki did it better than anyone expected him to. A polite observer might describe him as a player of modest skills. His range and arm strength are below average among major-league shortstops, and at that position, he often tries to compensate by taking a couple of crow-hops before releasing the ball toward first base. At the plate, he hits into ground-ball outs more often than not, except when he hits foul balls. His swing seems tailor-made for hitting foul balls.

Collectively, those foul balls can sometimes be an asset. Kawasaki appeared at the plate in the guise of a scrawny kid, the easiest out in the batting order, but he could drive a pitcher to distraction with his sharp eye and uncanny ability to extend at-bats by spoiling pitch after pitch. On April 17, for example, the Chicago White Sox told Jose Quintana not to waste pitches on Kawasaki after the number nine hitter worked the lefty for a six-pitch single and an 11-pitch walk in his first two trips to the plate. So Quintana challenged Kawasaki in his third at-bat and he singled on the first pitch to end the left-hander's night. Such peskiness led to a disproportionate number of walks and an on-base percentage roughly 100 points higher than his batting average.

KAWASAKI COMES FROM A culture that values conformity. A Japanese proverb warns: "The nail that sticks up gets hammered down." When he was a child, his elders often viewed him as an unwelcome joker in the deck of Japanese solemnity. "Somebody would say, 'Stop laughing, don't smile.' But I would forget about it and just continue smiling," he recalls. It helped, of course, that his baseball aptitude and work ethic extracted the most from his raw talent. It was easier to forgive a quirky, effervescent personality in a kid that could play.

"Everybody accepted him," says Suzuki. "At first, some people might be taken aback and say, 'Man, that guy's weird,' but he just makes them like him. It doesn't matter where it is — America or Japan. Even if he went to the Amazon, he'll be that same way and be accepted." Some insight into how much Kawasaki became accepted among the Blue Jays came June 25, when he was optioned to Buffalo to make room for Jose Reyes.

In the early afternoon, he stood at his locker in the far end of the visitors' clubhouse at Tropicana Field and donned a bright blue T-shirt inscribed with the same message in Japanese, Spanish, and English:

Jose Bautista signs autographs before a spring training game against the Baltimore Orioles on March 7, 2013, in Sarasota, Florida. Charlie Neibergall / AP Photo

Mark Buehrle warms up in the bullpen before an audience of minor-league pitchers at the Blue Jays training camp. John Lott

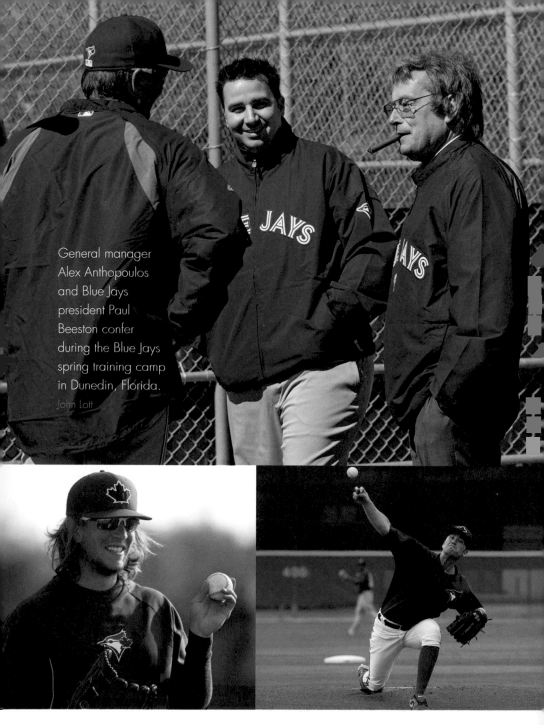

General manager Alex Anthopoulos and Blue Jays president Paul Beeston confer during the Blue Jays spring training camp in Dunedin, Florida. John Lott

Colby Rasmus shares a laugh with a teammate during a morning spring training workout. John Lott

Jays closer Casey Janssen warms up before pitching in a minor-league game on March 17, 2013. John Lott

Mark Buehrle and daughter Brooklyn parade Slater, their Staffordshire terrier, at the Jays spring training camp. Slater, who was rescued from euthanasia in Chicago, is banned in Ontario. John Lott

Detroit Tigers manager Jim Leyland and Blue Jays manager John Gibbons chat before an exhibition game in Lakeland, Florida, on February 23, 2013. John Lott

Jose Reyes seems to appeal for help from above during batting practice at the Rogers Centre. John Lott

Mark DeRosa plays air guitar on his bat during a Sportsnet video shoot under a massive tent in Dunedin, Florida. John Lott

R.A. Dickey fields questions during a news conference at the Rogers Centre on April 1, 2013, the day before his opening night start for the Blue Jays. John Lott

A crowd of 48,857 packed the Rogers Centre for the Blue Jays' home opener against the Cleveland Indians on April 2, 2013. John Lott

Jose Reyes, who sprained his left ankle during an April 12 game in Kansas City, watches his teammates from the dugout the next day. Reyes was out of action for nearly 12 weeks. Orlin Wagner / AP Photo

Toronto's Rajai Davis dives back to second base during the Royals' 3-2 victory over the Blue Jays on April 14, 2013, in Kansas City. Jeff Moffett / Icon SMI

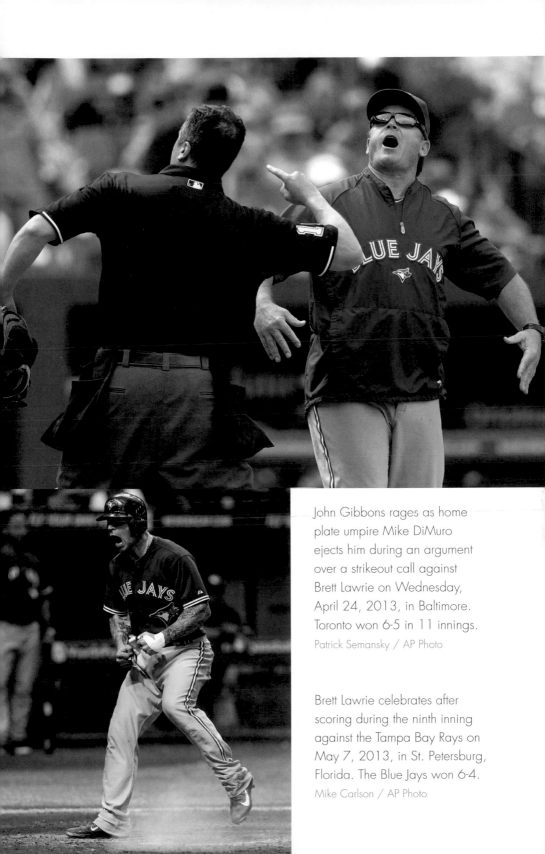

John Gibbons rages as home plate umpire Mike DiMuro ejects him during an argument over a strikeout call against Brett Lawrie on Wednesday, April 24, 2013, in Baltimore. Toronto won 6-5 in 11 innings.
Patrick Semansky / AP Photo

Brett Lawrie celebrates after scoring during the ninth inning against the Tampa Bay Rays on May 7, 2013, in St. Petersburg, Florida. The Blue Jays won 6-4.
Mike Carlson / AP Photo

Munenori Kawasaki admires the tattoos on Pablo "Panda" Sandoval of the San Francisco Giants during batting practice on May 14, 2013. John Lott

Emilio Bonifacio pretends to interview Kawasaki in the dugout before a game against the Tampa Bay Rays on June 25, 2013. Mark LoMoglio / Icon SMI

Kawasaki warms up before the Jays' game in Yankee Stadium on May 18, 2013. Kathy Kmonicek / AP Photo

Munenori Kawasaki talks to reporters at Fenway Park on June 28, 2013. He was recalled to the Blue Jays after just two days in the minors. Kyodo / AP Photo

Kawasaki stays loose before games with an unusual array of stretches and exercises, including handstands. He did this one during batting practice on April 17, 2013, in Toronto. John Lott

After defeating the Chicago White Sox 7-5 on June 11, 2013, in Chicago, the Jays celebrate the first victory of their 11-game winning streak. Paul Beaty / AP Photo

As umpire Marty Foster signals a fair ball, third baseman Brett Lawrie follows through on his throw to first base during a game against the Tampa Bay Rays on May 8, 2013, in St. Petersburg, Florida.
Mike Carlson / AP Photo

Edwin Encarnacion was the Blue Jays' top hitter in 2013, leading the club with 36 homers, 104 RBIs, 144 hits, a .370 OBP, and a .904 OPS. John Lott

Veteran Mark DeRosa (left) and Brett Lawrie enjoyed a mentor-pupil relationship (and a few laughs too) during 2013. Here they are before batting practice in Yankee Stadium on August 21. John Lott

Jose Bautista stretches before a game against the Baltimore Orioles on June 22, 2013, in Toronto. Chris Young / The Canadian Press

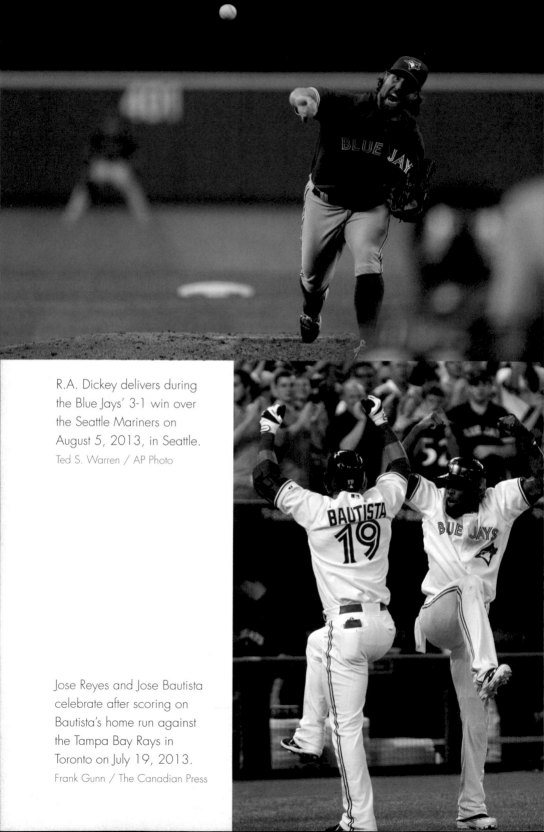

R.A. Dickey delivers during the Blue Jays' 3-1 win over the Seattle Mariners on August 5, 2013, in Seattle.
Ted S. Warren / AP Photo

Jose Reyes and Jose Bautista celebrate after scoring on Bautista's home run against the Tampa Bay Rays in Toronto on July 19, 2013.
Frank Gunn / The Canadian Press

Outfielders Rajai Davis, Jose Bautista, and Colby Rasmus celebrate their win against the Houston Astros on July 26, 2013, in Toronto.

Jon Blacker / The Canadian Press

Tampa Bay's Jose Lobaton ducks under the throw of Jose Reyes during the Jays' game in St. Petersburg, Florida, on Friday, August 16, 2013. The Rays won 5-4.

Jose Reyes lines a single to centre field against the Seattle Mariners on August 6,

"Let's go!" He was not in the starting lineup, but at 3 p.m. he walked down the left-field foul line carrying his glove, bat, and a set of strap-on weights. As he approached the foul pole, he leaned over the short wall, grabbed a folding chair, set it on the foul line, and sat down. He attached the weights to his forearms and, while seated, began the gyrations of his daily exercise routine. Next, he clamped the weights to his ankles and undertook another set of seated exercises. Twenty minutes later, he repaired to the batting cage under the bleachers to take his swings, and shortly thereafter returned to the field to stretch again on his own, before joining his teammates for the their collective stretching ritual.

He did not play in the game, but as always, he cheered for his teammates, so boisterously at one point that he drew a curious look from the home-plate umpire. Pitcher Mark Buehrle noticed that from the mound. He was used to Kawasaki's cheers. The umpire was not.

That night, after Toronto lost to the Tampa Bay Rays, John Gibbons called Kawasaki into his office. Following a brief conversation, they walked together down a short hallway and made a left turn into the clubhouse, where they stood side by side. The manager had an announcement to make. Jose Reyes, already in the clubhouse, would be activated from the disabled list the following day. Kawasaki was going back to Buffalo.

Buehrle, who had pitched that night, was deeply moved. The 14-year veteran had never seen a manager call the team together to announce a player demotion. "This is the part of the game that sucks," Buehrle said. "Between the fans and the guys in here, I think everybody's fallen in love with this guy." Later, speaking privately to a reporter about how much Kawasaki had meant to him and to the team, Buehrle's eyes were moist.

Gibbons acknowledged that he had never before called a meeting for this purpose. Kawasaki is special, Gibbons said. "He loved those guys out there as much as they loved him. But he'll be back, trust me on that one."

Kawasaki did return, just two days later, when Melky Cabrera landed on the disabled list. Two weeks later, he was again dispatched to Buffalo, with Gibbons promising again that he would be back. In mid-August he was, this time for good, after Bonifacio was dealt to the Kansas City Royals.

Before he left Tropicana Field that night in June, Kawasaki met with the media, assisted by translator Brad Lefton, who works for NHK-TV in Japan. "This one strange Japanese guy, [to] come here and be accepted the way I have, has really been an unbelievable experience," Kawasaki said in Japanese. When asked if he had a farewell message to the fans in Toronto, he did not wait for Lefton to translate the question.

"I am now hungry," he replied.

Tittering ensued among the gathered media. Kawasaki was doing his stand-up act again, they thought. Then, as Lefton spoke to him softly, Kawasaki's eyes widened and he laughed. He had not understood the question. This time his message for the fans came from the heart, not the stomach. "I love you guys," he said.

He further endeared himself to the fans after the August 16 birth of his first child, a son named Issho, in Toronto. When Kawasaki rejoined the team at Yankee Stadium a few days after the birth, a reporter reminded him that his baby was a Canadian. The new papa grinned. "He is Canuck, eh!" Kawasaki crowed.

"Oh man, the kid will be happy, I guarantee that," Gibbons said with a grin. "I met his wife earlier in the year. She seemed bubbly, too."

AS THE SEASON WOUND DOWN, Kawasaki's playing time dwindled. Reyes was ensconced at shortstop and rookie Ryan Goins, just up from Buffalo, was making a strong impression at second base. But Kawasaki was seldom far from the fans' consciousness. Late in a dreary loss on September 1, the Rogers Centre felt like a tomb until a single female voice screamed: "KA-WAH-SA-KEE!" The crowd cheered. An inning later, Gibbons sent Kawasaki in to pinch-hit and the fans were quickly on their feet, roaring. When he struck out, a sympathetic groan filled the stadium.

Munenori Kawasaki is the rare player loved more for who he was — for his unbridled panache and spontaneous joy — than for the numbers under his name in Baseball Reference. From a statistical perspective, Kawasaki might make it as a brief footnote in the history of the Blue Jays, if he makes it at all. But for a few months in 2013, he became the team's most beloved player, which was both a credit to him and a comment on the sad way the season was playing out.

THE SOCIAL GAME | 12

HE DIDN'T SEE IT COMING. J.P. Arencibia had spent most of three big-league seasons cultivating a cheery, charitable image, making himself a vanilla-flavoured Blue Jays ambassador and an undisputed face of the franchise. He achieved that status by hitting a lot of home runs, eagerly accommodating the media, serving as a conscientious team envoy at community events, and building an upbeat, fan-friendly Twitter account, @jparencibia9, that attracted more than 145,000 followers.

Then, in 2013, Arencibia made a misstep increasingly common among high-profile athletes who open themselves to the love and hate that wrestle relentlessly in the arena of social media. When criticism wounded him, he snapped back. Suddenly, in bizarre fashion, the once-merry catcher turned crabby, poking a media beehive. The result was predictable, perhaps to everyone but Arencibia. Casting himself as an indignant martyr, he fired clumsy counterpunches at his tormentors. Finally, he quit Twitter in a huff, his farewell tweet sending love to his supporters and prayers to his haters.

"It's unfortunate to see how words are twisted to make false stories," he wrote in a July 23 goodbye message that required three tweets. "I give way too much of myself to have others try and make me out to [be] something/someone I'm not."

The criticism that seemed to bother him most came from Gregg Zaun and Dirk Hayhurst, two former players hired to provide analysis of the Blue Jays for the assorted appendages of the Sportsnet media empire. Zaun had been a catcher, Hayhurst a pitcher. They had more than a passing knowledge of the job Arencibia was assigned to do, and they found him sorely flawed. Their acerbic analysis stirred echoes on Twitter and among callers to sports radio stations.

A fundamentally decent 27-year-old man whose tweets were generally inoffensive and occasionally clever and fun (in a hygienic sort of way), Arencibia seemed sincerely bewildered by the blowback when he and his team flopped in the face of lofty expectations. He took it as ingratitude for all he had put into his job and his efforts to attract fans to the Blue Jays. And even though there was little to be gained beyond some fleeting satisfaction, he could not resist the urge to fight back. It was so easy. He had Twitter, he had the airwaves, and he had the ear of every baseball reporter in town.

FOR THE TEAM, THE blowback began early. Gibbons was the easiest target; #FireGibby began to appear on Twitter by mid-April. As the month drew to a close, a fan tweeted: "So . . . when can I panic about the #Jays? Can't pitch, can't catch, no clutch hitting. Have to believe we're a week away from firing #gibbons." Many of the tweeters and radio-show callers said Gibbons was too laid-back. The Jays needed a manager who could light a fire under the moribund team, they insisted. Variations on the same message were repeated all year long, even during the team's few brighter periods.

It was another example of a classic 21st-century media phenomenon. Society in general has developed a chronic aversion to complexity. Simplistic thinking abounds, probably no more pervasively today than in the past, and probably no more frequently in the realm of sports than anywhere else. But simplistic "analysis" of sports-related issues seems more ubiquitous than ever, thanks largely to the knee-jerk, one-dimensional, largely anonymous criticism found on Twitter and in other social media, as well as on call-in shows that encourage listeners to embrace a binary view of the world. So if a team struggles in April under a new manager, the obvious solution is to fire him. The same talk-show hosts who hailed Anthopoulos as a genius in December were calling him a dunce in April, urging fans to call in and argue about it after the team had played 15 games. This is commonplace media clamour, of course, but its intensity was new for the Blue Jays. After all, they were supposed to be new and improved, and they decidedly were not.

As the losses piled up, players preached patience, but many fans were not in the mood. It is impossible to assess whether the views expressed on Twitter and call-in shows represented the larger fan base, but many public responses suggested a personal betrayal. Fans had been promised a winner. The Blue Jays had failed to deliver. Some said it looked like they weren't even trying.

"[The] guys *are* trying," 20-year veteran Darren Oliver said in late April. "But looking at it from a fan's point of view, I can understand that frustration. But as players, we're doing the best we can. It's not easy. Those other teams are out there trying to win just like we are."

Like Oliver, Casey Janssen said he paid no attention to the criticism. While both have Twitter accounts, which they rarely use, both said they weren't even aware of the fans' unrest. The naturally approachable Janssen often interacts cordially with fans in public settings. When told of attacks on Jose Bautista as he rested a back injury, Janssen pointed out a truism of Twitter.

"It's very easy to sit behind a mask, or a computer screen, and get real tough," he said. "Out in public, when it's one-on-one, it's not so easy. It's probably the absolute opposite. The same guy who's blowing Jose up [on Twitter] would probably die for a Jose Bautista signed bat, or a picture."

Many fans, of course, were more bewildered than bitter. Chris Jones, a Canadian writer for *Esquire* and *ESPN The Magazine*, summed it up well in a May 4 tweet: "The Blue Jays are a mathematical impossibility. How can 25 players be that bad at everything all at once?"

IF THERE WAS A single event — or tweet — that drove Arencibia from Twitter, it was not immediately evident. Perhaps wisely, he did not elaborate. In one of his last tweets, however, he lashed out at a couple of boors who were taunting his mother in the stands at a Blue Jays game. But he had a great deal more to say three weeks earlier when he blasted Zaun and Hayhurst for their recurring criticisms of his performance. On the evening of July 3, Arencibia used Twitter to announce that he would strike back the next morning during a radio interview on Sportsnet 590 The Fan. That done, he regurgitated his retorts to a media mob in a pre-game dugout scrum later in the day. A few hours later, Zaun and Hayhurst replied in a pre-game TV segment. This media circle game played out prominently on multiple arms of Rogers Communications, which owns the Blue Jays, Sportsnet, and The Fan, and employs Arencibia, Zaun, and Hayhurst. It probably didn't hurt ratings either.

Entering 2013, Arencibia seemed an unlikely candidate for such a sideshow. Over his first two seasons, he gave fans plenty of reasons to like him, on and off the field. He was young, handsome, and accessible. He earned a pass for his low batting average (.222 over two years) and on-base percentage (.261) because he was generally perceived as a hard-working up-and-comer who hit the long ball (35 homers) and drove in runs (101). But in 2013, the fans' forgiveness faded.

According to expectations, the Jays' revamped lineup would pack more punch and provide cover for Arencibia's sub-par stats while he continued to develop. Instead, his shortcomings became more conspicuous. His teammates did not produce, and, after a promising April, neither did Arencibia. As impatient fans lined up to take their shots, they no longer spared the catcher.

They had plenty of evidence. By mid-summer, statistics showed that Arencibia ranked among the worst catchers in baseball, both offensively and defensively. His home-run production had dwindled. His batting average was hovering around .200 and his strikeout total exceeded the sum of his hits and walks. The final numbers read: .194 batting average, .227 on-base percentage, 21 homers, 18 walks, and 148 strikeouts.

At least his retreat from Twitter offered him some protection. "I'm done with it," he told a *USA Today* reporter in late July, refusing to answer questions for a story on social-media pitfalls. When it appeared a few days later, the 1,575-word story began: "Toronto Blue Jays catcher J.P. Arencibia quit Twitter last week … "

During his very public tiff with Zaun and Hayhurst, Arencibia acknowledged that his positive public persona, on Twitter and elsewhere, probably served as a lightning rod when the critics started to pounce. "It's part of me caring so much," he said. He had gone out of his way to interact with fans, and the media, and sick kids, and what did he get? "Just constant pounding of the negativity," he said. As media-savvy as he had been, he simply could not comprehend how Twitter could turn on him so.

TWITTER BRINGS OUT THE best and the worst of the human condition, and Jose Bautista has seen both sides. In mid-April, when back spasms forced him to miss four games in a row, a fusillade of vicious tweets accused him of being soft and questioned his masculinity. Sitting gingerly in a chair by his locker, his back wrapped tightly in an elastic bandage, he joked that he was making a collage of the critical tweets, then admitted that he was sorely tempted to answer back in kind.

"The professional in me has to be polite and do things right," he says. "So I'm just going to let my playing dictate what I bring to the city and to this team."

But the attacks did not stop when he resumed playing. His batting average dropped to .195 on May 1, unleashing another torrent of venom. When Bautista retweeted some of the critics' taunts, sympathetic fans took to Twitter en masse to support him.

Bautista has more than 400,000 Twitter followers, but remarkably, he also follows more than 100,000 people, most of whom follow him. He has hired a team to manage his social media endeavours, and as part of their research they look for Bautista followers who fit a certain profile — people "that do love the game and follow the game and are true fans," and who are not inclined to nastiness, he says. The process helps keep things calm and generally positive.

Since hiring his social-media team at the beginning of the season, Bautista has found that his Twitter timeline has become far less confrontational. "Earlier on, I wasn't always following people that were true fans of either baseball, the Jays, or myself, and now that I do, I can kind of control a little bit more of the message that I want to put out there and the type of tweets that I want related to my name."

The change in tone helps him resist that temptation to reply to criticism he considers unfair.

"Even when I am struggling or the team isn't doing great, my feed is not flooded with nasty messages," he says. "Maybe those messages are still there, but I just get so many positive ones that I can't really see the others anyway."

AMONG THE BLUE JAYS, the Twitter fare is generally innocuous — playful jibes between players, inoffensive photos that show well-dressed boys being boys, and shots of baseball gear made by companies the players endorse. There is money to be made in tweeting, too, as many endorsement deals require players to send out a specified number of messages about a certain product. The connection between an athlete and his followers on Twitter is one highly coveted by marketers. But occasionally, when the critical feedback cuts close to the bone, a player feels compelled to return fire, as the combative Brett Lawrie did in May when Twitter fans started to pile on during his extended batting slump.

"All u people who chirp when things don't go good have never done anything in pro sport . . Ever . . So shut ur mouths #LetsGetThisThingg #jays," he tweeted. Shortly thereafter, he deleted the message, but not before it popped up for a fleeting moment in the breakneck daily news cycle.

"I expect a lot out of myself, but at the same time I'm not going to sit there and take all that from people that I don't know," he said when Brendan Kennedy of the *Toronto Star* asked him about his Twitter snit. "So if I want to say something back, I have more than the right to. Freedom of speech. People want to come at me with something, then I'm not scared to say something back."

But Lawrie's Twitter persona turned calm after that episode. Bautista, who has his own fiery side, said he does not actively counsel his teammates on how to cope with Twitter critics. But his experience has taught him that Twitter is a fountain fed by two springs, and at any moment, the sweet taste of positive reinforcement can turn to bile.

"It's a delicate subject and it's complicated," Bautista said. "And I don't want to say that my teammates haven't been good at dealing with it and I have been perfect. That's not at all what I'm trying to portray. I try not to get into fights with fans on Twitter and I think that's what everybody should do."

TWITTER MAKES IT EASY for fans to connect and criticize. But as Janssen observed, it also promotes the sort of uncivil discourse that most fans would not stoop to in a face-to-face discussion. Along with fame and wealth, criticism comes with the territory for professional athletes, but its sting can puncture players who deal daily with frequent failure in a fishbowl.

One Blue Jays player said he's seen in previous seasons how the steady stream of Twitter taunts can eat away at players and creep into the clubhouse as they discuss their frustrations. Players should not be on Twitter if they lack the discipline to ignore their mentions or if they simply cannot avoid taking the anger personally, he suggested. There is too much to be lost, too little to be gained.

Evan Longoria, the Tampa Bay Rays star third baseman, summed up many players' feelings in June when he tweeted: "For those who think it necessary to tweet athletes they follow when we fail, trust that we care more than u will ever understand."

That was one of the last messages retweeted by J.P. Arencibia.

But then, on August 15, @jparencibia9 re-appeared on Twitter with this message: *This is now the official FAN page for #BlueJays C J.P. Arencibia. Stay tuned for announcements, contests, photos & more — Posted by Team JP.*

Asked about the apparent change of heart, Arencibia said his agents were handling the account. "That's not me on Twitter," he said. "I'm not on Twitter."

But you had to authorize it, right?

"I had to authorize it because I had signed contracts," he said, briskly walking away from an interviewer.

"Team JP" would make sure Twitter became a vehicle to fulfill Arencibia's endorsement contracts. His next tweet promoted an autograph-signing session sponsored by a sporting-goods manufacturer.

13 | THE RETURN OF REYES

THE WALKOUT MUSIC JOSE Reyes used before his first at-bat during home games was "Started from the Bottom" by Toronto-born rapper Drake, its simple rags-to-riches narrative an apt anthem for the flashy Blue Jays shortstop. Born to a poor family in the impoverished Dominican Republic town of Palmar Arriba, Reyes grew up playing baseball with a milk carton on his hand, riding a donkey to and from the stone-littered local baseball field, the only one for miles around. Take away the fluid fast-twitch muscle movement, precise hand-eye coordination, and sprinter's speed, and he might have ended up working in a ceramics factory making toilets, as his dad did.

But as Drake would put it, now he's here. Those gifts, a diligent work ethic, and an effervescent disposition transformed Reyes into a four-time all-star who is one of the most exciting players in baseball, a multimillionaire who makes his own reggaeton videos as a hobby and wears flamboyant clothes while also helping the needy back home. He regularly distributes baseball equipment and athletic gear from his sponsors to local kids, while people seeking everything from money to buy medicine to food at Christmas time come to the same piece of land he grew up on, now adorned with new homes for himself and his family. "If I feel they're honest, I'm going to help them out," Reyes says. To borrow from another well-worn hip-hop theme, Reyes hasn't forgotten where he's from, either.

Still, the sprained left ankle he suffered April 12 in Kansas City meant his first season with the Blue Jays had only just begun in July, and by then "Started from the Bottom" was also shaping up as a potential narrative for his team. Having fallen flat in April, recovered mildly in May, and returned to level ground in June, the Blue Jays had essentially earned themselves a restart after their dismal opening.

Reyes, injured on a fateful slide into second base that tore up his ankle, rejoined the Blue Jays lineup on June 26, ranging far to his right on the first ball hit to him and firing a long strike to first base to nab the speedy Desmond Jennings. R.A. Dickey threw a two-hitter that day in a 3-0 win against the Tampa Bay Rays. Although the Blue Jays dropped two of three at Tropicana Field in that series, they were still 39-38 thanks to their recent 11-game win streak, and were ready to invade Boston for a potential statement series with the AL East–leading Red Sox. Even after they dropped three of four at Fenway Park to close out the month, the long-awaited return of Reyes — a putative catalyst on the field and in the clubhouse — helped renew optimism. Dickey opened July by baffling the hard-hitting Detroit Tigers for seven innings in a Canada Day matinee at Rogers Centre, Alex Anthopoulos was hunting for rotation help, and promise, however faint, was again in the air.

OPPORTUNITIES FOR A BETTER life were sparse as Reyes was growing up in Palmar Arriba, a tiny speck north of Santiago De Los Caballeros near the heart of the island nation. Everybody in the town knew each other, residents easily walked from one end of the village to the other, and the streets had no names. Reyes's father, Jose Manuel, worked long hours at a ceramics factory while his mother, Rosa, stayed home raising Jose and his younger sister, Miosoti. The family bungalow was short on luxuries — they slept on mattresses piled atop a concrete floor and the bathroom was out back — but the household was filled with joy and laughter. That environment is the reason Reyes looks like he never has a bad day.

Reyes started playing baseball at seven. Jose Manuel was a bit hesitant at first because his son was so much smaller than the bigger and rougher other kids. His father coached in the area and had played when he was younger, but wasn't especially gifted. He could run a little bit, but that was all. Reyes's maternal grandfather, Rafael Torrivio, on the other hand, was a pitcher and outfielder of some repute in local circles, although he never played professionally. The gifts Reyes inherited may have come from him, but honing that talent didn't come easily. The family couldn't afford a glove for young Jose, who instead used an old milk carton to help scoop grounders hit his way. He picked nearly every ball in range, anyway. Over time his father saved and finally bought Reyes his own glove. He was 12, and it didn't matter that it was used. "I felt like I got a brand new car," he says, smiling at the memory. "My dad, it was tough for him . . . but he was able to save some money and give me that gift. He was always there, supporting me."

By then, Reyes had started to gain notice. He was still small and he wasn't particularly fast, but he could field and hit. A year later, when a team from Santiago was in Palmar Arriba for a game, the visiting coach, a man everyone called Moreno, watched Reyes and was impressed. He pulled Jose Manuel aside afterward and told him his son had real talent, but needed to play in Santiago's city league to test his ability against better competition and get more exposure. Jose Manuel was reluctant. Each taxi ride to and from Santiago would cost the family money they couldn't spare. Reyes was hesitant, too, because all he had known were the people of Palmar Arriba, and they didn't "associate with too many people from the city and stuff like that," he says. "I didn't want to go because I was happy in my city, but [Moreno] explained to my dad what that could bring to me in the future. My dad decided I'd go there for a little while and see what happens. Thank God."

What happened was that Reyes blossomed in the Felix de Leon league, batting third for his team while sparkling on defence. But he was still small and skinny, weighing 130 pounds as he approached his 16th birthday. Moreno told him he needed to show the visiting scouts more. "At that time I had a little bit of speed, not too much, and he said it would be a good idea for me to be a switch hitter," says Reyes, who also focused on getting faster. "My town has a lot of mountains. I didn't run up, I ran down, that's where I got my speed. When you go up, it gets your legs too strong, they get heavy. I still go there and run in the off-season."

The extra effort paid off, eventually. Shortly before he turned 16, the Marlins invited Reyes to work out with them for a week but declined to sign him. Same with the Chicago Cubs, who didn't think he could succeed as a switch-hitter. Later that summer, the New York Mets worked him out. Scout Eddy Toledo was captivated. "There was something special in his face and eyes," Toledo told *ESPN The Magazine* in 2006, and that prompted him to project how Reyes's energy would enhance what were then average or below-average tools. "Eddy was in love with me. He said, 'We're going to sign you right away,'" recalls Reyes. "One of the happiest moments of my life, right there."

The session with the Mets started at 10 in the morning, and by noon some of Reyes's friends ran to his father at the ceramics factory to update him on how well the tryout was going. "They told my dad, 'I think they're going to sign your kid,' and my dad was going crazy," Reyes says. "He ran away from his job, came to meet me, and then I got signed. He was happy, very proud." The Mets offered $13,500, which to the Reyes family was life-changing money. He signed on August 16, 1999 — the first player from Palmar Arriba ever to sign a professional contract — and his first thought was to take care of his parents. "They deserved to be comfortable," he says. "When I got the cheque, I sent it to them and said, 'Start building a new house because you guys have been everything for me.'"

Rather than starting him in their Dominican academy, as is typical for most young Latin players, the Mets pushed Reyes right into the North American arm of their player-development system and the following summer he made his pro debut at Kingsport of the rookie-ball Appalachian League. He had just turned 17 and was terribly homesick, but batted .250 in 49 games with a .359 OBP and 10 stolen bases. "The first year I came to the States, I didn't want to go because I was, 'How is it going to be, I don't speak the language, I'm not going to be with family anymore,'" he says. "Kind of a tough transition. But I passed." Did he ever. Three years later on June 10, a day before his 20th birthday, Reyes made his big-league debut for the Mets at the Ballpark in Arlington, collecting a single to right field off John Thomson in his first at-bat and later doubling and scoring in a 9-7 loss to the Texas Rangers. Two years later Reyes led the National League in stolen bases for the first of three straight seasons, and a year after that, in 2006, he was an all-star for the first time, his personality as engaging as his play. A video-board skit at Shea Stadium entitled "Learn Spanish with Professor Reyes" played on his efforts to pick up English, with the shortstop "teaching" people in the stands. "That was the Mets' idea, the fans fell in love with that," he says with a grin. "Even players on the other teams watched." Fans loved his flash, talent, and style, and everywhere he went fun followed.

FOR THE BLUE JAYS, the promise in late June quickly changed to pessimism in July. The team's fortunes turned drastically and dramatically after Dickey's gem against the Tigers. They opened the second game of their series against the eventual American League Central champions with a four-run first off Doug Fister, but Chien-Ming Wang failed to survive the second inning for a second straight start, pulled after a Detroit six-spot. The Blue Jays quickly tied it, but squandered chance after chance before falling 7-6. The Tigers won more convincingly the next two nights, including an 11-1 thumping in the finale, and suddenly baseball's hottest team was back in a slump, cooled by a 3-8 stretch against three legitimate contenders. Though the Blue Jays recovered to take two of three from the Minnesota Twins before hitting the road again, they went 2-4 through Cleveland and Baltimore before the all-star break, again failing to make up ground on teams ahead of them in the playoff race. Worse, they were giving back all the ground they had made up during their 11-game spurt, and the questions were mounting.

Wang's too-good-to-last comeback story ended after the Tigers thrashing. Tossed into the rotation in his place was journeyman minor-leaguer Todd Redmond, who had all of one big-league start to his name. With Josh Johnson still a mess, Brandon Morrow a distant hope, Ricky Romero going sideways at Triple-A Buffalo, and J.A. Happ needing more rehab time, it wasn't a promising promotion (although Redmond ultimately fared far better than anyone expected). Dickey remained enigmatic, following up two of his better starts with duds against the Twins and Indians. Only Mark Buehrle and Esmil Rogers, pitching like an ace until the Tigers strafed him on July 4, were offering any kind of consistency. But it couldn't fall only to them to pull the Jays out of their funk.

Toronto was 45-49, 11 and a half games behind John Farrell's first-place Red Sox in the AL East and eight and a half games out of a wild-card spot as the baseball world descended upon Citi Field for the all-star game. Despite their lowly standing, the Jays had four all-stars in New York — Jose Bautista, Edwin Encarnacion, Brett Cecil, and Steve Delabar. Manager John Gibbons was there, too, chosen as a coach by Tigers manager Jim Leyland, who was running the AL squad. Only Detroit, St. Louis, Baltimore, and Pittsburgh — all contenders — were better represented. "We're totally capable of playing a lot better baseball than we've shown," Bautista said during all-star media day. "We just need to play better as a team. I'm number one on that list. I've been very inconsistent this year, and I need to pick it up some and bring that consistency I know I can bring to the table, and bring more steady production and help the team win more games." While more offence would help, that wasn't what the Blue Jays most needed at that point. "I think the starting pitching," Encarnacion said when asked to identify the team's biggest weakness. It was an honest assessment of his teammates in the rotation. "If we want to win, we know and they know we need to pitch better."

But with only 68 games remaining and multiple teams to leapfrog in the standings, the Blue Jays were out of margin for error. "We need to do something quick to be realistic. We don't want to kid anybody," Gibbons said. "We need another nice long streak and to definitely start playing some better ball." Then he reprised a sentiment he had expressed as far back as April. "I still like this team, I really do, and I've seen us get on a roll. If we hadn't had that 11-game win streak, that's a totally different story, but I've seen what we're capable of. You still have to go out and do it."

For the Jays who were not part of the all-star festivities, the break represented a chance to recharge after a frustration-filled first half. Reyes remained in Toronto with his family and used the time off to rest his ankle, which remained troublesome. In his first 18 games back, Reyes posted a .746 OPS with three homers, seven RBIs, and 14 runs scored, but he stole just three bases in four attempts, and looked tentative while rounding bases. He grimaced noticeably while slowing down after a sprint, and balls hit to his left in the field often sneaked through. Despite the special brace he wore to stabilize the ankle, it was clear he wasn't totally right, and probably wouldn't be until after a full off-season of healing.

REYES'S LEFT ANKLE FIRST became an issue back in 2003, when he suffered a Grade 2 sprain sliding into second base trying to break up a double play in August. That injury abruptly ended his rookie season and led him to abandon feet-first slides in favour of head-first dives into the bases. And while it didn't keep him from swiping bags almost at will, it did mark the first of many ailments to plague him as a Met.

In 2004 he missed time with a strained right hamstring and a stress fracture in his left fibula, while in 2009 he went on the DL with right calf tendinitis, then tore his right hamstring in September and later underwent surgery to clean up scar tissue in his right knee. In 2010 he missed time with a hyperactive thyroid and a strained right oblique, while in 2011 there was tightness in his left hamstring to contend with. That's why his current daily regimen to keep his legs healthy starts six hours before game time and includes roughly 90 minutes of massage therapy, hot and cold tub soaks, and special strengthening exercises.

The Mets learned to live with the injuries, an unfortunate accompaniment to his dazzling play on the field. Reyes stole 60, 64, and 78 bases in 2005, 2006, and 2007 to lead the National League, while hitting the most triples in 2005, 2007, 2008, and 2011. In 2008 he also led the NL with 204 hits. In a city where Yankees superstar Derek Jeter was king, Reyes was popular enough to make a legitimate run at the crown.

However, there were low times too, most notably during the Mets' historic collapse of 2007, when they blew a seven-game lead in the NL East with 17 games to play, ceding the division title to the Phillies on the final day of the season. Reyes batted just .187 during that stretch with two homers, seven RBIs, and 11 runs scored, and was booed heavily while going 0-for-5 in the season finale, an 8-1 loss to the Marlins. Afterward, he stated the obvious: "They wanted me to do good, so that's why they booed me." The Mets made the playoffs just once during Reyes's tenure. They lost in Game 7 of the 2006 National League Championship Series to the St. Louis Cardinals.

By the time Reyes, the face of the franchise, became a free agent after the 2011 season, the Mets were in major financial distress that forced them into rebuild mode. The Miami Marlins, entering their new ballpark, made him one of their key off-season targets, and met with him at a New York hotel the minute free agency opened. They signed him to a $106 million, six-year deal December 9, 2011, while the team that had lifted him off the island and developed him into a star never even made direct contact, let alone an actual offer. "I can't be crying about that, because they didn't show me anything," Reyes said after joining the Marlins. "They didn't push anything to have me there. Why should I worry about it if they didn't want me? But I appreciate they gave me the opportunity to play professional baseball and play in the big leagues."

Reyes joined Mark Buehrle and Heath Bell at the centre of a rare Marlins winter splurge. With an impressive cast of incumbents already in place, including Josh Johnson, Anibal Sanchez, Hanley Ramirez, and Giancarlo Stanton, contention seemed like a sure bet. Instead, with manager Ozzie Guillen contributing to the fiasco with some ill-advised comments praising Fidel Castro (a huge no-no in a community thick with Cuban exiles), the Marlins were a disaster from the outset and stumbled to a 68-94 mark. Guillen was fired three weeks after the season ended, and while Reyes didn't think the roster would remain intact, he never thought he might be part of the turnover. After all, he had assurances from the very top. "Jeffrey Loria [the Marlins owner] always told me he's never going to trade me," says Reyes. "He always called my agent and told him, 'Tell Jose to get a good place here to live' and stuff like that." Happy in his 5,000-square-foot mansion in Manhasset, N.Y., Reyes never did buy a home in Miami, even after an early November dinner in which Loria again broached the subject. Shortly thereafter, Reyes and his wife left for a vacation in Dubai. They had barely arrived when he awoke to a stream of text messages telling him of the trade to the Blue Jays. "I thought people were joking about it. I called my agent and he said, 'Yes.' It surprised me a little bit but it's time to move on," said Reyes, who insists Loria never made any mention of a potential trade during their dinner. "He was talking still about getting a nice house in Miami. That was kind of crazy. How you want me to spend money in Miami when I have my house in New York, and you're going to trade me in two days? . . . After the trade I didn't talk with those guys [in Miami's front office]. I don't need to talk to them because if they traded me, I don't need to talk to them."

FOUR GAMES AND FOUR losses into a crucial stretch of their second half, the Blue Jays players decided that they needed to talk. Coming out of the all-star break with renewed optimism, they continued to find the ground covered with upturned rakes to step on. They were swept by the Tampa Bay Rays right out of the gate before a five-error mess led to a 14-5 clubbing by the Los Angeles Dodgers. With hopes for a turnaround slipping away by the day, a 70-minute, players-only meeting was held the next afternoon, with the focus on playing a better quality of baseball to the very end. "There are guys in this room that genuinely care about the season, care about each other," said Casey Janssen. "We're kind of tired of seeing the product that we're seeing on the field." Adam Lind summed up the major talking points succinctly: "Stick together. Let's grow up a little bit. Let's play baseball like grown men." One player who preferred anonymity said the meeting was professionally handled and positive. "There was no finger pointing," he said. He added that the clubhouse atmosphere was healthy at the beginning of the month, but deteriorated quickly after that. He thought the meeting might help. Another player said, "Guys were honest with each other. I felt like everybody could speak their piece without worry of a fight breaking out or anything like that. [It wasn't] where guys really didn't enjoy being around each other and they were looking for reasons. It was open floor and guys were able to say what they want."

Anthopoulos also felt the meeting was a good idea but admitted to pulling the plug on trade talks for players to help out in 2013. He had been keeping close tabs on Jake Peavy, but pulled back. The White Sox later traded him to Boston. Anthopoulos was still aggressively looking to make moves for '14 and beyond, but his efforts to land Hisashi Iwakuma and Kyle Seager from Seattle went nowhere. The July

31 non-waiver trade deadline was looming, and the GM said, "I really don't see us doing anything." They didn't.

Right after the meeting, the Blue Jays led the Dodgers 8-3 through six innings, then collapsed and lost 10-9. The next night they blew a one-run lead in the ninth when Colby Rasmus misplayed a bloop single, then surrendered a five-spot in the 10th in an 8-3 loss that gave the Dodgers a sweep. Thankfully for the Blue Jays, the Houston Astros were next up. Toronto took three of four from baseball's worst team before embarking on a 10-game road trip to the west coast. They took two of three from the AL West–leading Oakland Athletics, finishing July at 10-16. The Blue Jays opened August by losing three of four in Anaheim to the Los Angeles Angels, rallying late in the series finale to avoid a sweep, but any thoughts of a miracle turnaround were extinguished for good.

The usually positive Reyes finally showed his exasperation after the Jays blew a late lead in a 7-5 loss to the Angels on August 2. "It's tough to play the way we've been playing," he said. "It's not acceptable with the kind of team that we have. We're better than this." Expanding on his comments the next day, Reyes added, "No disrespect to some other teams, but we have more talent than some other teams who are playing for first place, playing better than us. We feel like we have more talent, but we haven't been able to put it together on the field."

And having lived through a season of disappointment in 2012 with the Marlins, he was loath to be doing it again in 2013 with the Blue Jays. "There's no doubt in my mind [that the 2013 Jays] are much better, way better [than the 2012 Marlins]. We came with high expectations here. We haven't been able to do anything. It's disappointing because it's unbelievable talent that we have here. But here we are into August, we're in last place, and we expected to be on top of our division coming into spring training.

"We had a lot of opportunities to win a lot of ballgames and we just let it get away. That's not going to get it done."

Indeed not. Not only had the Blue Jays started 2013 at the bottom, it was clear they were destined to stay there. And Reyes was correct: too many players with impressive histories had failed to measure up. The team so craftily assembled in November and December was far less than the sum of its parts.

14 LEARNING HOW TO LEARN: BRETT LAWRIE

ON THE NIGHT OF May 24, John Gibbons and Brett Lawrie sat in the manager's office and watched their team on TV. Both had been ejected in the third inning, Lawrie for objecting to a called third strike, Gibbons for rushing to Lawrie's defence. Thus banished, they shared a black leather couch for several innings and watched another Blue Jays loss unfold.

"We talked about different things, what happened with the umpire, how you should react," Gibbons recalls. "I understand the frustration. Sometimes in this game you have to snap. There's nothing wrong with that. You just can't do it all the time."

Ironically, this was one of Lawrie's milder outbursts. Before his ejection, he didn't say a word in protest. He did flip his bat and helmet in disgust and, as he walked away, tossed his batting gloves behind him toward the plate, where umpire Dan Bellino was standing. Bellino apparently concluded that Lawrie was throwing down the gauntlet and dismissed him from the game. Lawrie said he was simply flipping his gloves back toward his bat and helmet for the bat boy to collect. Crew chief Wally Bell later offered a quaint explanation for Lawrie's transgression: "He threw [the gloves] back toward Danny in a way that wasn't etiquette in baseball."

Two days later, it became clear that Gibbons's chat on the couch had not covered etiquette of another kind. Miffed that his fly ball to right field had not brought in a runner from third base, Lawrie glared at the third base coach, Luis Rivera, and the runner, Adam Lind, as if to suggest they'd taken leave of their senses. (It seemed obvious to everyone except Lawrie that Lind was slow afoot, the right fielder had a strong arm, and running would've been foolhardy in the face of a two-run deficit.) When Lawrie reached the dugout, still fuming, Gibbons remained seated but lit into him for showing up his coach and a teammate. Lawrie shrugged and snapped a defensive reply. "That's bullshit," Gibbons barked, wagging his finger. The manager's rebuke continued in that vein before Jose Bautista spoke quietly but firmly to Lawrie and quickly escorted him away, ensuring the televised confrontation did not escalate.

Lawrie apologized in a team meeting the next day, but made no public comment. The incident served to reinforce his reputation as an *enfant terrible*, a 23-year-old package of raw energy, extraordinary talent, and bullheaded self-absorption tied to a short fuse. "I ain't changing," he had vowed in a 2012 spring training interview when asked about his reputation for rubbing opponents (and occasionally teammates) the wrong way. And over parts of two big-league seasons he had fulfilled that promise. Sometimes it begat brilliance, especially on defence. Sometimes it led to an ugly scene (as it did in 2012 when he slammed his helmet to the ground and watched it bounce up and hit an umpire who had just called him out). Sometimes his impulsive baserunning hurt his team. But even when he made an obvious mistake, he was loath to admit it. "I was just trying to help my team win," he often said when reporters asked about such gaffes.

Two incidents early in the 2013 season cast the Lawrie legend in bold relief. On April 20 in the 11th inning, he charged a bunt when he should have been covering third base. Pitcher Aaron Loup fielded the ball, turned, and threw, believing Lawrie was where he was supposed to be. It was a play often practised in spring training. But this time,

Lawrie was out of position and Loup's throw sailed past him. Two Yankees scored. The Jays lost 5-3. Afterward, Lawrie took no responsibility. His odd, ambiguous response was: "The throw was already on its way. Not throwing Loup under the bus, but I think I could've been back." It was a *non sequitur*. He *did* throw Loup under the bus, and he *should* have been back.

The other incident came a month later, when he provoked his manager and teammates with the public show of pique at Rivera and Lind. The Blue Jays came back to win that game on a Munenori Kawasaki double, taking some of the focus off Lawrie's moment of petulance. But the next day, he left it to teammates to tell the media that he had apologized. Many fans felt he had dodged public accountability for a public misdeed, and insisted that discipline — benching or worse — was warranted. Lawrie was also batting .199 at the time, making his insolence even harder to forgive.

The next day, he sprained his ankle sliding into second base. He would miss seven weeks.

When he returned, Brett Lawrie began to change. The message he'd heard in various ways from various people finally took root. His rough edges were holding him back. He needed to calm down and grow up.

"If everybody's telling you the same thing, maybe they're right," Gibbons says. "Sometimes when one guy tells you something, you take it with a grain of salt. When everybody's telling you, maybe there's something to it."

Three men were principals in the alchemy that put Lawrie on a new path: Mark DeRosa, Chad Mottola, and Edwin Encarnacion.

DEROSA WAS CONTEMPLATING RETIREMENT in January when Alex Anthopoulos called. A 15-year-veteran who played for nine teams that went to the playoffs, DeRosa was approaching his 38th birthday and wondering whether a team would want him, especially after a spate of injuries had sabotaged his once-respectable batting stroke. Never a star, DeRosa was a smart, blue-collar player who extracted the most from his talent by becoming a diligent student of the game and seeking advice from more accomplished teammates. "I never was good enough not to keep learning the game," he says.

Anthopoulos offered DeRosa a job. The GM needed a 25th man for his 25-man roster, a utility player who would seldom play. He also liked DeRosa's reputation as a respected leader in the clubhouse. There was something else too: DeRosa was to serve as guru for Brett Lawrie. The job paid $750,000. DeRosa agreed. When he reported for spring training, Lawrie's locker was next to his.

"With Brett, I could tell as soon as I walked in the clubhouse what kind of personality I was dealing with — a high-energy guy with a lot of talent, and not a lot of desire yet to really want to sit down and grind out every aspect of the game that I wanted to help him with," DeRosa says.

Lawrie had been a can't-miss prospect since his teenage years in Langley, B.C. His father, Russ, started putting Brett and older sister Danielle through rigorous daily baseball drills while they were in elementary school. Danielle became a professional softball pitcher, Brett a first-round draft pick of the Milwaukee Brewers in 2008. Traded to the Blue Jays in winter 2010, Lawrie drew raves from management during spring training as he began the conversion from second baseman to third baseman.

By 2013, he had become reliable, and occasionally spectacular, at the hot corner. But after wielding a hot bat when he was called up for two months at the end of 2011, his hitting levelled off to .273 in 2012. He missed nearly all of August of that year with an injury and batted only .237 over the final month.

In spring training, the mentorship Anthopoulos had envisioned quickly began to blossom. Fifteen years apart in age, DeRosa and Lawrie became fast friends, on and off the field. Before the exhibition games started, they played baseball in the mornings and golf in the afternoon.

"I felt like on the golf course the two of us could get in the cart for three and a half, four hours, grab dinner afterward, and [I could] really get a chance to know what his mom and dad were about, what his sister was about, and what his past was about," DeRosa says. "What was he as a 12 year old? Was he the greatest Little League player ever? Some guys, mentally, have never failed. I wasn't that guy. So I wanted to get to know him. And once I felt I got to know him, there could be moments where I could be honest with him, where he knew it's coming from a good place. 'This guy knows me as well as anybody on this team. If he's saying something, or correcting me, or giving me a piece of advice, maybe I should at least digest it.'"

DeRosa picked his spots. Some were obvious. When Lawrie refused to admit he was wrong on the bunt play, and when he showed up Lind and Rivera for depriving him of an RBI, DeRosa was there to calmly pass on wisdom gained from playing more than 1,100 games in the big leagues. He talked about being a good teammate as well as being a good player. He talked about accountability.

"If you're going to be a leader — if you're going to be a guy that this franchise dubs bobblehead-worthy — you're one of the faces of the franchise," DeRosa says. "You need to take accountability when you mess up. We're human beings. We're going to make mistakes in this game. We're going to cost our team games. It's the way the game is. It's a game of failure. But I think for him, in his maturation process, he needs to know he's got to be held to a different standard than a lot of guys. He's one of the cornerstones of this franchise, and if he can be around here and get this team to where he wants it to go, and I know that's the World Series, then he's got to be accountable."

And that meant Lawrie had to break his habit of denying his misdeeds. He had to own up. Says DeRosa, "The fans respect you. Your teammates respect you. You lose so much more than you win by denying."

After spraining his ankle, Lawrie was gone for all of June and the first two weeks of July, first undergoing treatment at the Blue Jays' complex in Dunedin, Florida, then playing minor-league games on a rehab assignment. When Lawrie rejoined the Blue Jays, DeRosa noticed a change.

"He actually turned to me one night at dinner and he asked me, 'What's the one thing I need to do to get better?' I said, 'Your passion and energy that you play with on defence is what makes you a Gold Glover. Your passion and energy when you're at the plate is what's killing you. So if you can change that guy from there to there, keep turning him on and off, you're going to be unbelievable. But until you relax at the plate, you're never going to be as good as you can be.'"

To that point in his career, Lawrie had relied on his natural skill and instincts and assumed they would always be enough. That night at dinner, DeRosa says, "I think he realized he was going to have to make a change."

LAWRIE'S BATTING STANCE SERVED him well as a member of Canada's junior national teams and in the minor leagues. There was a feral quality about the menacing crouch, the hectic bat-waving, and the pronounced leg kick that set up his swing. The stance was the embodiment of Lawrie himself — edgy and untamed. And in 2013, it began to turn on him.

Chad Mottola knew Lawrie well. He was Lawrie's hitting coach at Triple-A Las Vegas in 2011, and in 2013 they were reunited in spring training when Mottola took over as the Blue Jays hitting instructor. One morning, as Mottola was setting one ball after another on a tee so Lawrie could practise his swing, the coach began to fear for his own safety. "He was almost hitting my hand before I took it away from the tee, he was so anxious, so eager," Mottola recalls.

Like Lawrie, Mottola had been a first-round draft pick, but he played only 59 games in the big leagues. However, he spent 16 years in the minors, playing 1,800 games, the final 340 with the Blue Jays' Triple-A team in Syracuse. The Jays were so impressed with his hitting acumen that they gave him a minor-league coaching job immediately after he retired as a player in 2007. Within two years, he was the Triple-A hitting coach, building a reputation as a smart, patient tutor who fostered a productive rapport with his hitters. The Cleveland Indians thought highly enough of him to interview him for their hitting coach job before the Blue Jays promoted him to their big-league staff for the 2013 season.

He knew he'd have to be patient with Lawrie. "His whole life, and in the minor leagues, he was the best player on the field, and he never had to listen to anybody," Mottola says. "The way I like to see it is, he had to learn how to learn, and that's where he was early in the year. He didn't know how to apply some things. He understood what I was saying but he never had to make adjustments."

In spring training 2013, an oblique injury forced Lawrie to miss almost all of the exhibition games. After joining the Jays on April 16, he batted below .200 for almost two months, then got hurt again on that slide into second base. When he returned, Mottola saw the same change that DeRosa had noticed. Lawrie was ready to learn.

Mottola told him he had to cut down on the bat waving. The more Lawrie moved his hands, the higher his leg kick rose before he swung. Quieter hands would calm the rest of his body and reduce the height of his kick, curbing his tendency to lunge at the ball. And if the changes didn't work right away, Lawrie had to overcome his natural tendency to fight himself.

"In knowing him well over the years, and having the relationship we've had, he knows that I know his swing," Mottola says. "Sometimes he gets so angry, he can't hear. But we knew if we controlled his hands, it would control his lower half."

The changes did not bear immediate fruit — Lawrie struggled for the last two weeks of July — but he took off in August, batting .346 with a .946 OPS. His calmer approach also helped improve his patience at the plate. Through July, he had three strikeouts for every walk. In August, he had seven of each.

While Mottola focused on the finer points, DeRosa stressed a macro message: to stick in the majors requires constant adaptation and study. Lawrie took it to heart.

"This game's tough and it's all about trying to find a way to get it done without just repeating the same [mistakes] over and over again," Lawrie says. "Everyone's adjusting. The other team's adjusting, I'm adjusting, because you get exposed so quickly here. Mark told me that they're just going to keep exposing stuff. When I got back from my injury, I just started to find a little bit of a different way, slowing the game down a little bit at the dish, trying to just keep everything calm and just use my hands, because I've got great hands."

The early reviews on Lawrie's new approach were positive, but it is too soon to conclude that stardom lies just around the corner. He is far from a finished product. He cooled off in September, batting only .243 with a .304 on-base percentage. He still waves the bat too much for Mottola's taste. "Sometimes he never gets to the point where he gets relaxed because he does that too long," Mottola says. In spring training of 2014, the coach had planned to work on that, and try to convince Lawrie to focus less on results in exhibition games and more on refining his hitting mechanics. His message: "It's not about [the results] after 20 at-bats. This is about a 10-year career, a 15-year career, so let's build slowly and figure out who you are." Mottola wouldn't get the chance to help anymore. Eight days after the season ended, the Jays announced they would not renew his contract for 2014.

EDWIN ENCARNACION STRUGGLED MIGHTILY — on offence and defence — after the Blue Jays acquired him in a 2009 trade with the Cincinnati Reds. He was a wild-armed third baseman whose offensive shortcomings became so glaring in 2010 that he was sent to Triple-A Las Vegas. It was a wakeup call. His exile lasted only a week, and it was probably a coincidence that during his time in the desert he worked with a hitting coach named Chad Mottola. But when he returned, he started to hit. Encarnacion enjoyed a breakout season in 2012 and carried that momentum through 2013, ranking as the third most productive power hitter in baseball, behind just Miguel Cabrera and Chris Davis, based on home runs and RBIs.

A generally reserved man, Encarnacion seemed an unlikely tutor for the loud and brash Brett Lawrie. But it was Lawrie who sought Encarnacion's counsel. In an offence that sputtered all season, Encarnacion was a model of consistency. They began to watch video of opposing pitchers together.

"I went to him because he's doing something that all of us aren't, so he's got to be doing something beneficial," Lawrie says. "He's just a good hitter. He's got a great approach towards the game, and when he steps in the box, he has a great mentality about what the pitcher's going to do. So I figured I need to step into that approach as well."

Encarnacion welcomed him. "I like when young guys ask me questions and they want to learn, especially a player like Lawrie. He's got great talent and he's going to be a good player. The same thing he's asking me I asked people before, veteran players like [Albert] Pujols and Aramis Ramirez. I asked them what they do to prepare their minds for the game. I feel like when I was a rookie player, I asked them because I wanted to learn."

Studying video is only one component of a hitter's preparation, but it is essential. As DeRosa says, "You can't just go up there and leave it to the gods." Not only does video help a hitter identify the types of pitches a pitcher throws, it also helps him to identify tendencies.

Says Encarnacion: "I like to see what they're going to throw when they're ahead in the count, when they're behind in the count, when they have two strikes what they like to throw, do they like to throw inside, do they like to throw outside, all that stuff."

During the two-plus seasons they were teammates, Encarnacion says he and Lawrie were friends, but never discussed hitting. So he was impressed when Lawrie came to him for help in the video room.

"When players like him ask something, they want to learn, they want to be better players. I said to him, 'You're not going to start hitting because of [watching video].' No. He's hitting because he has his timing. You need to have your timing. If you don't have your timing, you're not going to hit. But [watching video] gives you an idea of what the pitcher will throw to you. So when you go to the plate, you go with a plan."

Suddenly, the high-octane young Canadian, his quick-twitch muscles swathed in tattoos, had a quieter presence at the plate and a more studious approach to hitting. This, from the impetuous kid who once vowed, "I ain't changing."

"My attitude toward the game, and the way I play, I don't think that's changed," Lawrie says. "I still have that same mentality." But he adds this too: "You've got to use your teammates. I've got teammates who have had a lot of success in this game. They're doing something that a lot of us aren't, so I'd be stupid not to keep my ears open and go up to them to see what they have to offer."

His mentors say they believe Lawrie turned a corner in 2013. And in the process, he raised his defensive bar a notch, bringing fans to their feet with dazzling plays night after night. One of his best came on August 30, when he charged a one-bouncer that took a high hop at the last second. He had to jump and bare-hand the ball, unleashing the throw before his feet hit the ground. His quick throw to first beat the runner. It looked like something out of *The Matrix*. "I've always been relatively athletic, I guess," he says, nodding in the general direction of modesty.

"The way he started the season and the way he is now, he's grown up a lot," says infield coach Luis Rivera. "The main thing is he's slowing down the game — ground balls, everything, the game is slowing down. It's part of maturity in baseball. And I think DeRosa's also doing a terrific job with him, talking to him every day, taking ground balls with him and guiding him."

Lawrie says he sees a lot of himself in DeRosa: "We hit it off just like that because he's got that energy and that enthusiasm, just like I do."

DeRosa: "I think Brett and I are very different in a lot of ways, obviously, but very similar in our passion. We just have a little different way of showing it. He reminds me of my football buddies that I grew up with, guys that would run through a brick wall for you. You just have to tell them what times to do it and what times not to do it."

Lawrie: "He's just fun to be around. He's 38 but he acts like he's my age."

DeRosa: "I don't like to say he was at a crossroads at 23, but I saw a guy who believed he was better than what he was showing. And it was time. I didn't learn how to hit until I was 30. He's learned at 23. I think the sky's the limit when he fully gets a couple times through this league and really knows himself."

ASSIGNING LAWRIE AND DEROSA to adjacent lockers and letting nature take its course was one of the few Blue Jays success stories in 2013. From their first day together, the kid and the veteran liked each other, although they seemed an odd couple. Lawrie, a British Columbia amateur phenom, hit the pro ranks at 19 and reached the majors at 21. At the same age in 1996, DeRosa was a former Ivy League quarterback and business-school graduate from the University of Pennsylvania who was starting his professional baseball career in Eugene, Oregon, the lowest of the low minors. DeRosa made seven stops in the majors before he was hired, in part, to play shrink, foil, and friend to Brett Lawrie. It was no act. They clicked.

Critics have reason to question the judgement of Alex Anthopoulos for his high-profile moves in the winter of 2012. But one of his footnote transactions definitely paid off. Mark DeRosa helped make Brett Lawrie better.

UP FROM THE UNDERTOW: R.A. DICKEY

A FEW DAYS BEFORE R.A. Dickey tried to swim across the Missouri River, he asked fellow pitcher Grant Balfour to give him a haircut. Balfour, a native of Australia, was the Nashville Sounds' unofficial team barber during the 2007 season. He called his specialty the Brisbane Fade, and Dickey got one. Now Balfour was desperately trying to give Dickey a hand, hopping a fence and racing along the east bank of the Missouri River, trying to keep up with the ruthless current that was hauling Dickey downstream. If only his teammate could swim close enough to shore, Balfour might be able to reach him.

"You could tell that the undertow was pulling him," says Balfour, now the closer for the Oakland A's. "He was really struggling. It was a really strong current. It got a little scary."

The Sounds are the Milwaukee Brewers' Triple-A farm club, and the two right-handers were working to revive their careers that year. During a series with the Omaha Royals, the Nashville team was staying in Council Bluffs, Iowa, at the Ameristar Casino Hotel, about a 10-minute bus ride from the Royals' stadium in Nebraska. The Missouri River forms the border between the two states. Dickey decided to swim to Nebraska.

On previous road trips, Dickey had surveyed the river from his hotel room and contemplated the challenge. Now, he decided, the time had come. For anyone, not to mention a 32-year-old man with a wife and three kids, it was a foolhardy notion. But Dickey had just entered a new phase of upheaval in his troubled personal life. Only recently he had summoned the courage to tell a trusted counsellor about the sexual abuse he had suffered; at age eight he was abused several times by a 13-year-old female babysitter, and shortly thereafter by a 17-year-old male. While Dickey was starting to find some success with his knuckleball, he worried that his baseball career might last only until the Brewers needed to clear the next Triple-A roster spot. "I think I was really searching for validation of some kind," he says. It was a crazy idea, but he thought he might find validation in the river. A scattering of teammates stood on the bank to watch him try.

Exhausted as he neared the middle of the river, Dickey felt the sudden grip of the undertow and decided to turn back. As his flailing strokes grew weaker, he became certain he would die in the filthy, roiling water. He began to cry. "It's a very odd sensation, weeping in water," he wrote in his autobiography. "I am filled with contrition."

"I could tell he needed help," Balfour recalls. "I just remember going down there, kind of on instinct. I got in the water a little bit and stuck my arm out."

Dickey's feet hit bottom in about eight feet of water. He bounced up, breathless, and summoned the strength to swim a few more strokes. Then he saw Balfour and reached out. Balfour helped him stagger up the bank, where he collapsed. "He had a little panic to him," Balfour says.

As Dickey, clad in muddy boxer shorts and tank top, headed back to the hotel, his teammates laughed and joked about his escapade, as teammates are wont to do. They knew nothing of the turbulent personal journey that nearly ended a few minutes earlier.

"He never talked about stuff like that. I think that's something that he had hidden," Balfour says. "He was a great guy, good teammate. I was only with him for a few months, but we had a lot of fun."

With time, Dickey has come to better understand what drove him into the murky current. He says he was still in transition from his old, sometimes reckless, baseball-focused existence in which he tried to act the part of the intrepid jock while repressing the dark fears from his past that kept gnawing at his present. He had begun to move forward through painful but productive counselling and a renewed religious faith. But he still self-identified as a baseball player, measuring his worth by his success on the mound, and now he sensed that his career could slip away at any moment.

"And so I thought I could do this great feat," he says. "Perhaps I could be remembered for something. I think it was centred around the last remnants of my old self, trying to find an identity outside of the game. That's the psychological analysis of it. On the surface I think I was just trying to do something special because I felt so unspectacular in every other area of my life."

His muddy swim on that June day in 2007 was hardly a proud moment, but it was an important step in the process that would pull his life, as well as his career, out of the muck.

"I'm completely embarrassed that I ever tried such a ridiculous feat," he says. "But then again, if I wouldn't have, I don't know if I would've had some of the epiphanies that I did."

AS AUGUST 2013 BEGAN, Dickey continued to search for an epiphany on the mound. Like the Blue Jays, he was in salvage mode. In 2012, he had been a sensational pitcher on a bad team, one of the few sources of pride for Mets fans, a knuckleball pitcher who finally and remarkably hit his stride at age 37. He won 20 games, posted a 2.73 ERA, and led the league in strikeouts. In the voting for the Cy Young Award, he was a runaway winner.

Now, Dickey found himself on a bad team once again, but this time he too was enduring a season of struggle. Entering August, his record was 8-11, his ERA 4.66, his strikeout total far off his 2012 pace. On the other hand, he and Mark Buehrle had become the bullpen's best friends, the only Jays pitchers who consistently worked deep into their starts. Both hit their stride in August, combining for a 2.89 ERA and an average of seven innings per start.

But for the team, August brought more gloom and a startling array of injuries. Reliever Dustin McGowan went down with an oblique injury on July 30, and by August 21, seven more players had hit the disabled list, including two of the team's most productive hitters, Jose

Bautista and Colby Rasmus. The other opening-day outfielder, Melky Cabrera, landed on the DL with a knee injury on August 1. A month later, tests revealed a benign tumour in his lower spine, the likely cause of his season-long leg problems. He underwent surgery to remove the growth on August 30. On the same day that Bautista left a game in Yankee Stadium, in pain from a bone bruise on the neck of his femur, Maicer Izturis suffered an ankle injury. Both were done for the season. Steve Delabar missed the month with a sore shoulder and fellow reliever Juan Perez suffered a season-ending elbow injury, two more signs of attrition among an exhausted bullpen corps.

And starter Josh Johnson was finally, almost mercifully, finished for the season with a forearm strain. Nine months earlier, the 6-foot-7 right-hander was the general manager's primary target in trade talks with Miami; now he was a millstone, his Toronto career possibly over, his legacy a 2-8 record, a 6.20 ERA, and a $13.75 million hit on the payroll ledger.

Meanwhile, R.A. Dickey was collecting a $5 million salary and conducting another in a series of experiments with the release point in his delivery. By the end of August, he was clearly on the right track.

AT AGE 30, DICKEY was facing the end of his pedestrian tenure with the Texas Rangers in April 2005 when he was summoned to the office of manager Buck Showalter. Waiting with Showalter were pitching coach Orel Hershiser and bullpen coach Mark Connor. They had seen Dickey fooling around with a knuckleball. Now they were telling him that his fool-around pitch represented his only chance to achieve success in the big leagues. The Rangers had given up on him as a conventional pitcher, but they saw something special in him as a person. They liked his grit, his intelligence, and his willingness to take a risk. They wanted him to succeed. "R.A. is such a personable and honest guy that we had a deeper relationship than just having a normal pitching coach/pitcher relationship," Hershiser said in a 2012 interview with *ESPN The Magazine*.

Showalter, who now manages the Baltimore Orioles, smiles when he recalls that pivotal meeting with Dickey. To convert from conventional pitcher to knuckleballer, a pitcher needs five qualities, and Dickey had them all, Showalter says.

"He's got to be a failed pitcher in the big leagues, not the minor leagues. He's got to have had a taste of failure in the big leagues.

"He's got to be athletic.

"He's got to have an existing knuckleball.

"He must be ready for it mentally.

"He has to have good, strong nails."

"IF A GUY'S BITING his fingernails, he's out," Showalter continues. "And there's also weak nails. They bend easily. Let's face it, R.A. blows out a nail warming up, he's done. One of the biggest things is his manicurist. You've got to be a tough guy, but you've got to be comfortable with a manicure."

Dickey has occasionally needed a manicurist (a knuckleball pitcher grips the ball with his nails, not his knuckles), and he keeps a glass nail file handy too, but those other qualities were more important. He certainly had known failure in the majors; his ERA was 5.33 in his previous two years with Texas. His fastball velocity was falling. Now his only chance was to start over, facing another long road with no guarantees, while throwing a pitch that precious few pitchers had ever been able to harness.

"He had the mental toughness to go through the failure," Showalter says. "You've really got to give in to it. You've got to take your ego out of it. And he knew things weren't going to get better the conventional way. He wanted to pitch in the big leagues. He had guts. And it didn't happen that a week later he was successful. He fought the fight."

It took five years.

SALLIE GIBBONS, THE MANAGER'S mother, says she is not a "groupie" baseball mom. Only occasionally does she tune in to a Blue Jays game in her San Antonio home. "Sometimes I watch on TV if it's on, and I'll just look to see if he's smiling," she says. "If he's smiling and he's happy, I think that's good."

It was not good in August, and in some ways, it was getting worse. Throughout the month, as the "fire Gibby" calls grew louder and the injury toll mounted, his team continued a pattern of playing close games and coming up short. Nine of their 17 August losses were by one or two runs. The Jays re-invented rock bottom when they lost four times in three days in Yankee Stadium, blowing a lead in each game. In the last three, the scores were 3-2, 4-2, and 5-3.

"It's frustrating," Dickey said after pitching eight innings in the 4-2 loss. "It's like the *Twilight Zone*. Different day, same script."

It marked the fourth straight close game in which Dickey had pitched at least seven innings. Twice in a row he had entered his last inning having allowed two runs, only to give up two more. In both of those games, opponents had scored the winning runs in their final at-bat. "It's really a very fluky kind of feeling," he said.

For the Blue Jays, it was no fluke. It was a habit.

After hip pain forced Bautista from an August 20 game in Yankee Stadium, the Jays lost seven in a row. Before leaving New York for Houston, Gibbons suggested they detour to Williamsport, Pennsylvania, site of the Little League World Series, "and hope for a split."

He said it with a trace of a smile, but there were no TV cameras, so his mom couldn't see it.

A WEEK BEFORE DICKEY was traded in December 2012, he represented the Mets at a children's Christmas party sponsored by the team. The New York media also came to the party and cornered the club's star pitcher to ask about his protracted talks with management about a contract extension. After five so-so seasons as a knuckleballer in the minors, he had finally harnessed the pitch and enjoyed three productive years in New York. But contract negotiations were not going well. He told reporters that his demands were more than fair and that he would likely leave as a free agent after the 2014 season if he could not work out an extension. None of this was surprising, given that the Cy Young Award winner was contracted to play in 2013 for $5 million at a time when the average big-league salary was $3.44 million.

But some critics chided Dickey for using a kids' Christmas party to sound off about his contract demands. And on December 16, the day before the trade to Toronto, Ken Davidoff of the *New York Post* went further in a scathing column that suggested Dickey and his well-publicized narrative annoyed some of his teammates.

"Dickey can be a handful," Davidoff wrote. "He clearly has enjoyed his rise from the ashes into a Flushing folk hero, and while he deserves praise and riches, there's also the matter of him having to coexist peacefully in a workplace. His gift for self-promotion and his love of attention don't endear himself to most teammates. Instead, his durability and outstanding results led him to be appreciated but far from beloved."

Without addressing the irrelevance of being both appreciated *and* beloved by 24 teammates, Dickey did concede that he should not have talked about his contract at a kids' party. He later apologized publicly, claiming he was unprepared for a scrum in that venue, but the attack wounded him. "That was just sad to me," he said in a conference call after the trade to Toronto. "I didn't feel smeared necessarily, because I'm confident in who I am and the things I do and who I am as a human being."

It was indeed a smear, of course. And it would be no surprise if the Ballad of R.A. Dickey had begun to sound off-key to some players. After all, baseball is a hidebound culture, full of enormous egos buffeted by repeated failure. "This game can humble you," players often say, in a provincial version of "pride goeth before a fall." Dickey had the ego and had experienced plenty of failure; for some critics, however, he simply wasn't humble enough. And, they felt, he talked too much about himself and issues beyond baseball.

Of course, he talked, in part, because reporters asked him to; he had become a media magnet. By virtue of his nature, background, and the pitch he throws, Dickey is a different sort of baseball player. He is smart and articulate. His backstory is unique and compelling, and when asked, he is not reluctant to talk about it. He often says he loves "narrative," and he clearly enjoys his own. In spring training, a few Toronto writers dubbed him "the most interesting man in baseball," an homage to the bearded renaissance man in the beer commercials.

Apart from his erudition, Dickey throws a unique pitch. His cultivation of the knuckleball to save his career paralleled a personal transformation that saved his life. After a series of spring-training interviews, most Toronto reporters moved on from his personal odyssey, but the knuckleball, which can turn from friend to fiend in an instant, remained a season-long story, especially because of the ordeals Dickey encountered as he tried to harness it in a new league, a tough division, and a home park notorious for giving up home runs. While other pitchers spoke in straightforward, clichéd terms about missing their spots with a fastball or a slider, Dickey spun tales of a "capricious" knuckleball, which darted and dived and then didn't, missing bats for long stretches and then flattening out and inviting a home-run swing that often turned a Blue Jays lead into a deficit. This singular, volatile, defiant pitch, and the vivid and intimate way he talked about it, sustained the Dickey narrative during his first season in Toronto. "You never master it, just to be clear," he said after his last start of the year. "It's certainly a pitch that you have a relationship with more than you master. For me, I've always felt like I've had the aptitude, thankfully, to be able to apply things in the middle of a game, in the middle of a season, to try to get better." The pitch was a parable, the perfect vehicle for a pitcher who once imagined a career as an English teacher.

"I love writing and the written word," he told a group of kids in August. "I think there's something pretty awesome and permanent about the written word." He also sprinkles his conversation with words seldom heard in a clubhouse environment. During one of his first media scrums in spring training, Dickey used "anomaly," "purview," and "correlation" as he spoke about his knuckleball. One night in August, he overheard a writer using "churlish" in a clubhouse conversation with a colleague. "Churlish," Dickey said quietly as he walked past. "What a good word."

It was a good word to describe the way many fans were feeling about the Blue Jays in August. With six games left in the month, the team was 16 games below .500. Then they went on a rare spree, winning five of six. Dickey and Buehrle each won two low-scoring games in that stretch.

Throughout August, no day passed without a sports talk-show focusing on whether Gibbons should be fired. The manager said he was unfazed. "My life's good," he said, insisting he deserved another year at the helm. "I enjoy competing every day out there . . . Really, what's there to fear?"

On the afternoon of August 27, Alex Anthopoulos announced that Gibbons would return to manage the Blue Jays in 2014. "To sit there and say it comes down to one person and that's the panacea, that just doesn't make any sense," said Anthopoulos. Firing Gibbons would be "an easy out," he added. That night, the Blue Jays lost to the Yankees for the 13th time in 2013.

NO ONE COULD REASONABLY expect Dickey to match his spectacular stat line of 2012, but his performance over the first half of the 2013 season represented a precipitous decline that few would have forecast. Through his first 17 starts, his ERA was 5.15. He had surrendered 17 homers, including 10 at home. For much of that period, however, he had not been entirely healthy. In his second April start, spasms in his right shoulder blade began to radiate pain into his spine, forcing him to alter his delivery mechanics to curb the discomfort. He did not miss a start, but his velocity was down and in three of his outings in May he was hit hard. Among the second-guessers in the fan base, he was twice cursed: for pitching poorly, and for continuing to pitch when he should have been on the disabled list. In fact, he said, a similar injury when he was a conventional pitcher in Texas did force him to the DL, but as a knuckleballer, he was able to keep pitching. When the spasms finally subsided for good in June, he had to readjust his mechanics in a bid to revive his 2012 form. And as his home-run totals soared, especially in the Rogers Centre, he decided to try something new.

A year earlier, he had learned to elevate his knuckleball just enough to entice frequent strikeouts. That became his "put-away" pitch. Now he was either missing the strike zone, or watching it flatten out on its way in and leave the ballpark on its way out. So he decided to focus on the basement instead of the attic.

"In years past I've been able to elevate my knuckleball pretty well," he says. "That was a key for [2012]. I would get a lot of swings and misses, which I do still, but it's the ones that stay up here [chest high] that are fly balls in other parks but are home runs at home. So I think, for my put-away knuckleball, which was the high knuckleball last year, I might need to make an adjustment and try to get them to chase it down and out of the zone."

It took constant tweaking of his release point, but gradually, it began to work. Over his next 13 starts through the end of August, his ERA was 3.34. Since mid-April, his knuckleball velocity had risen two miles per hour to 77.7, his fastball 1.5 miles per hour to 84. Both pitches almost precisely matched their average speeds of a year earlier.

By month's end, Dickey's knuckleball velocity was ranging from 65 to 82 miles per hour within the same game. He said he was feeling as strong and confident as he had during his Cy Young season, except for one nagging detail: "I've just been giving up home runs still." He'd allowed 29 in 29 starts, and finished with 35 in 34.

IN 2012, DICKEY WON a Cy Young Award, promoted his bestselling autobiography, started work on a children's version and a film adaptation of the book, and climbed Mount Kilimanjaro to raise money for a charity in India that rescues women and girls from sex trafficking. Two years earlier, after his first of three good years with the Mets, he had discussed his outside interests with general manager Sandy Alderson. What he was doing was unconventional for a baseball player, and he wanted to make sure his boss was on board.

"I was at the place in my life where I felt like I was starting to live differently than I ever had, and enjoyed it," he says. "More than enjoying it, I felt like it was instrumental in my development as a human being. I think it would be tragic if the only thing I was ever known for was being a baseball player. So I let him know that sentiment, and I kept him in the loop about everything that I was doing — the book, to the climb of Kilimanjaro, to supporting charities, to doing whatever. And he was great. I had a great relationship with Sandy. He's somewhat old school in that if he didn't think I could handle it he would've spoken to me about it."

Dickey's outside interests helped him to maintain balance in his life. He used to bring his work home, he says, and it was not a healthy time for him or those close to him.

"I'm not one of these guys that leaves the ballpark, goes home, locks himself in the room, and watches his highlights or his lowlights until he has to go to work the next day, trying to figure it out," he says. "I trust that I'm going to be able to figure it out because I work hard, and I apply myself, and I'm in the moment with what I do. But when [the work day] is done, I like to be able to leave it at the ballpark.

"It helps me. It helps my family. There was a time when I couldn't do that, and it was bad. I'd bring it home, I'd rage, I'd get angry, I'd be short with my wife, I wouldn't want to play with my kids, I'd be depressed, all those things. Those were manifestations of how I used to be before I really had more of me, and really understood that I had more to offer than just being a baseball player."

On a particularly dark day when Dickey was the way he used to be, he duct-taped a rubber hose to the exhaust pipe of a car, fed it through the driver's window, rolled the window up, packed a towel in the space around the hose, climbed in the car, and placed his fingers on the key. Suddenly, he says, he sensed that God was sitting in the passenger seat, telling him not to turn the key. God had work for him to do, Dickey says.

The gradual, painful, and ultimately uplifting change in his personal life began when he opened up about the toxic parts of his past. Eventually, that led him to the liberating experience of writing his autobiography with journalist Wayne Coffey. Reaching that point "took a lot of learning," he says. "I was brought to the end of myself, literally, before I came to that place."

Before he reached that place, Dickey viewed his life through the prism of a macho sports culture he had embraced since childhood. It was a façade, but he had made it work for a long time.

"I would project that I was this strong guy that could handle everything, do everything," he says. "It was all going to be okay because at the end of the day I was going to have all the answers. That's what I would project, but inside I was very broken and damaged and had a lot of toxic things going on. I eventually had to look that in the eye, and when I did, I discovered that my flaws and my mistakes and the things that I wasn't good at, if I was going to admit those things and try to get to the other side of it, I could grow. And that was the process for me. But those things in particular [were hurtful], especially to people that were close to me — my teammates, my wife, my kids in the early part of our marriage and the early part of their lives. Especially my oldest when she was three, four, five, and six years old, I wasn't very good at being a dad. I wasn't very vulnerable. I wasn't very transparent, and now I'm much more transparent than I've ever been. I feel like that's been big in her development as well as my own."

Stephen James, a counsellor in his hometown of Nashville, was the first person Dickey told about his childhood abuse. Later, Dickey told his wife, Anne, and his mother, with whom he had started to build a strong relationship after her recovery from alcohol addiction. He also told the minister of his church and several close friends. All helped guide him on the path out of the darkness.

"I can't express to you enough how instrumental other people were in my life. I didn't do any of this alone. If I would've been left to my own devices, I would be dead. Literally, I'd be dead. So it took a lot of people who loved me well. That, coupled with a fuller understanding of my faith, and with the help of the people who gave me the courage, who sat with me in my grief and in the things that were painful to look at that I had done, and that had been done to me, I started to grow out of it. But it's taken a long time."

THE BLUE JAYS FINISHED August with a 12-17 record. The bullpen, which had been the team's salvation for much of the season, was exhausted; relievers were charged with nine of the 17 losses. For the month, the Jays averaged 3.79 runs per game. Their opponents averaged 4.86. Their margin of error was roughly a run per game.

Dickey and Buehrle were bright spots. So was Brett Lawrie, who finally calmed down in the batter's box and heated up at the plate, batting .346 with an .892 OPS, all the while assembling a highlight reel of dazzling defensive plays at third base. Bautista was having a solid offensive month before he got hurt. Edwin Encarnacion, the team's steadiest hitter and most dependable power bat all season, cooled off a bit but still hit five homers and drove in 15 runs. He also drew 22 walks, in part because opponents could pitch around him with Bautista no longer in the lineup.

The Jays unloaded Emilio Bonifacio, one of the players acquired from Miami, to Kansas City for a player to be named later or cash. Batting .218 with a .258 OBP when he left, Bonifacio reported to the Royals and immediately turned into the player Anthopoulos had envisioned in November. While batting over .300, Bonifacio stole more bases in three weeks for Kansas City than he had in four and a half months for Toronto.

Dickey enjoyed his best month to date as a Blue Jay: a 3.07 ERA, 44 innings pitched, and 38 strikeouts. Meanwhile, he was reading (Tim

O'Brien's 1990 novel *The Things They Carried*, a bestselling collection of Vietnam war stories), writing a children's book, and talking to abuse survivors and educators about his experiences.

When the Jays visited Yankee Stadium in April, *New York Daily News* writer Andy Martino interviewed Dickey about his parting with the Mets and the sniping about his high-profile, multifaceted presence that followed. Some people in the Mets organization, Martino wrote, felt that Dickey should just shut up and pitch.

"That's just very barbaric," Dickey replied. "You're not allowed to have an independent thought? I think that's hysterical."

Dickey loves the baseball life and the opportunities it has afforded him and his family. He is a teammate, which requires a degree of cultural conformity. But he no longer worries about fitting in, about simply shutting up and pitching.

"I got to the place where I felt like I had something to say," he says. "If people liked it, great, and if they didn't, that was okay, too. I just feel like we all have gifts that we're given, and there's no reason for me to be ashamed of those, whereas before I kind of tiptoed into them. Sometimes I would even deny that I had a passion for things because of what it might look like in the eyes of somebody else. I felt like I cheated myself out of a lot of moments that could've been far richer."

Writing his autobiography has led to many rich moments, some within his own family. (He and his wife, Anne, have two girls, 11 and 10, and two boys, seven and two.) His eldest daughter has read the children's version of his book. That led her to ask, early in the 2013 season, whether he and Anne "almost got a divorce."

"We had a great conversation around that, about how marriage is hard, and how I made a lot of mistakes, and Mom made a lot of mistakes, and this is what it takes to really commit to another person," he says.

"She probably won't get the meat of that conversation until she's years down the road, but just to get to spend that time being vulnerable with my daughter, you can't replace it, or manufacture it, or fabricate it. It's organic. It's awesome."

Meanwhile, the Blue Jays of 2013 were still fighting the undertow in hopes of finding validation, however small, in the final month.

A BUNCH OF BROTHERS | 16

FOUR RELIEVERS SAT IN a circle in front of Casey Janssen's locker, talking quietly, their faces impassive. Each had pitched in the game that just ended, a 4-2, 11-inning loss to the Boston Red Sox on August 13. It was the Blue Jays' fifth defeat in six games and the fourth time in that span that a reliever was charged with the loss. Aaron Loup, the sixth of seven Toronto relievers that night, had surrendered a decisive two-run single to Shane Victorino.

Afterward, Loup, Brett Cecil, and Brad Lincoln pulled up chairs around Janssen. The bullpen men are a tight-knit group, and Janssen, the closer, is a quiet leader. Such post-mortems are not uncommon, he says. But they typically take place out of sight of reporters, who stood a few feet away on this occasion, gathered for the usual parade of post-game scrums.

"We were tired," Janssen says. "It was just a frustration, pump-up talk."

They had been tired for a while. All season, the early exits of the Blue Jays starters had put extraordinary pressure on the relief corps, which tied for the second-most innings pitched by any major-league bullpen. They held up remarkably well in the first half, but the heavy workload began to take its toll.

"We were just sitting there and almost laughing at each other," Janssen says. "It was kind of just par for the course, how well we've all pitched [earlier in the year] and how difficult it is right now to get three outs. It's just kind of the way the game swings. When you're going good, you're going good, and when you're not going as good, three outs seems like a tall task. The only thing we can do is sit here and joke and smile about it, because we know it's going to swing back in our favour at some point, and people are going to joke, 'The game's not that easy. How are you making it look that easy?'"

That's what people were saying during the first half of the season, when the bullpen was the club's only consistent bright spot, compiling a 2.90 ERA. (In June, its 1.16 ERA was the best in baseball.) Often, of course, its fine work did little more than contain an opponent that already had a lead. The Blue Jays seldom mounted a winning rally late in a game — they finished 9-68 when trailing after seven innings.

RELIEVERS ARE THE MOST obscure, fungible players in professional sport, and they are paid accordingly. Bullpen turnover is high; an adage among general managers is that a reliever who has a good year is expendable because he is unlikely to follow it up with another. Closers are the exception, but often their shelf life is relatively short too. That's why Shawn Camp, a former Blue Jays mop-up man, regularly described himself and his colleagues as baseball's pond scum.

So when the season opened, few critics had much to say about the Jays bullpen. Cecil, a failed starter, barely made the team out of spring training. Loup was an unknown when the Jays called him up in July 2012 after he found sudden success in the minors with a new sidearm delivery. Steve Delabar was a former substitute teacher with a steel plate and nine screws in his surgically repaired arm who resurrected his career when he discovered a weighted-ball training program. Neil Wagner and Juan Perez were hard-throwing no-names in the Triple-A bullpen at Buffalo when summoned early in the season.

And then there was Janssen, hardly the prototypical closer, who began doing the job by default when Sergio Santos, acquired from the White Sox following the 2011 season, missed almost all of 2012 with a shoulder injury that required surgery. Janssen took over in May that year after Francisco Cordero faltered as Santos's first replacement. In Janssen's 22 saves, he did not allow a run. After the 2012 season, he too needed shoulder surgery, described as a minor cleanup hardly worth mentioning.

But no shoulder surgery is insignificant; the consequences are always unpredictable. In the season following shoulder surgery, a pitcher often endures a year of frustration because his shoulder lacks its old zip and his velocity drops one or two miles an hour. He can pitch, often with respectable results, but the long-term healing process means the shoulder simply doesn't feel as strong. It sometimes takes the pitcher longer to get loose when he warms up, and longer to recover after pitching in a game. The changes are subtle and variable, but one thing stays the same: when he reaches back for that extra mile per hour, it isn't there.

So it was for Janssen in 2013. Because he had been rehabbing in the off-season, he could not follow his normal winter conditioning routine, and he had to take it slow in spring training. "I love to go-go-go. It kills me to not be in the games," he said. He pitched in only two exhibition contests, but after a period of uncertainty about whether he'd be ready to start the season, he broke camp with the team and saved its first win April 4.

Janssen had been through this before. In 2006, his rookie season, he started 17 games, then moved to the bullpen the next year and appeared in 70. Warming up in spring training 2008, he felt a searing pain in his shoulder. Surgery ended his season before it started. When he returned in 2009, his fastball velocity dropped more than a mile an hour, but he regained it the following year.

In 2012, Janssen's fastball averaged 91.7 mph. In 2013, following off-season surgery, it averaged 90, occasionally hitting 91 late in the season. One mile an hour may appear miniscule, but over the 60 feet, six inches from the mound to home plate, it can be the difference between a weak ground ball and a line drive in the gap. And especially early in the season, Janssen's lower velocity bothered him. So did his shoulder.

"It's a grind," he said in late April. "There's days when it doesn't feel great and there's days when it feels okay."

Janssen and his bullpen mates still weathered the grind and

achieved remarkable success in the first half. At the all-star break Toronto relievers led the American League in innings pitched — "Not a good recipe for success," says Pat Hentgen, a former Cy Young Award–winning pitcher who served as the team's bullpen coach. In the first half of the season, Janssen pitched in 32 games, logged a 2.76 ERA, and saved 18 wins in 19 opportunities. His fastball velocity may have been average by big-league standards, but he had a curveball, a slider, a cutter, and a changeup, and on most days he could locate them with uncanny accuracy. He worked quickly. He fielded his position exceptionally well. And he diligently studied video and scouting reports of opposing hitters, planning his attack strategy well ahead of time. "It's a mind game," he says. "It's a strategic game."

Meanwhile, he was trying to avoid looking at the scoreboard when it flashed the speed of his pitches. "You've got to pitch with what you've got," he says. "To look at the miles per hour is deflating enough, so I've stopped doing that. You've just got to pitch, and you read swings, you read the hitters' reactions and make pitches with your off-speed pitches."

Closers in the classic mold bring heat in the mid-90s. They keep batters off balance with a slower breaking pitch. Some throw an occasional changeup. Janssen's recipe for success contains more ingredients. "Casey's not the overpowering two-pitch type closer, but he gets a lot of strikeouts," Hentgen says. "He's a strike thrower. He catches guys looking. He locates four or five pitches really well. He's not afraid to pitch inside. He can hold runners. He can field his position. All those things add up to being a really good closer."

IT WAS INEVITABLE THAT some of the relievers would wilt, and remarkable that it didn't happen sooner. Delabar (1.71 ERA at the break) and Cecil (1.94) each pitched in the all-star game on July 16. By then, Delabar's shoulder was starting to ache; he spent August on the disabled list. From the break through the end of August, Cecil's ERA was 6.75, and after an outing in Houston on August 24, he leaned down to tie his shoe and felt a pain that ran from his triceps to his elbow. The pain, diagnosed as nerve inflammation in his elbow, disappeared with treatment and rest, but it returned in mid-September. Cecil was done for the season after pitching in 60 games in his first full season as a reliever. Juan Perez did not allow an earned run in his first 14 games, then allowed 13 in his next five and tore an elbow ligament. Providing late-season help was Santos, who had missed three and a half months following an April elbow surgery. At least one reliever was fresh, and Santos, at last, was behaving that way on the mound, taking on increasingly high-stakes assignments. "In the last two months, I really feel like the fastball has been coming out better and better, my command has been getting a little bit better," says Santos. "I finally feel now that everything is really close to where I was, hopefully even better."

In early September, the rotation enjoyed a stretch of long starts and the expanded roster allowed the Jays to add several pitchers to share the bullpen burden, bringing relief to the relievers. The bullpen's ERA ballooned to 4.36 over the July–August period; in September, it fell to 3.63. "It's been kind of a grind at times," 42-year-old Darren Oliver understated. "It's not a grind now. We've got a lot of reinforcements. There were some moments when we got a little taxed down there."

HENTGEN SAYS THE LEADERSHIP of Oliver and Janssen helped keep the relief contingent positive during an extraordinarily gruelling season. "The guys have done a really good job all year of picking each other up and passing the baton, rooting for each other, trying to learn from each other," he says.

Heading into retirement after a 20-year career, Oliver says he will miss the bullpen camaraderie more than anything else. Because their work routine is separate from everyone else on the team, relievers form a special bond. In the afternoon before a game, they stretch, run, and throw in a group. When the game starts, they leave the rest of their teammates behind and set up shop in a coop behind the outfield fence. "It's like a family," Oliver says. "Like a bunch of brothers."

The relievers of 2013 were exactly that. "A great group of guys," Oliver says with a smile. "We've had a lot of fun, regardless of the [team] situation. We're out there all by ourselves, except for Pat. The first time the phone rings, that's when it gets real. But before that, we're telling stories. We're not just talking about baseball, we're talking about everything — what's going on in the world, other sports, family stuff, just like you would do in a regular job."

THE BLUE JAYS DRAFTED Janssen in 2004 and brought him to the majors as a starter in 2006, during Gibbons's first term as manager. In his rookie year, the club won 87, lost 75, and finished second, 10 games behind the Yankees. That was the best team Janssen has played on. So he was among those particularly disappointed that the 2013 Blue Jays did not measure up to off-season expectations. As the longest-tenured player on the roster, he acknowledged that he gave his share of "pump-up" talks to his teammates. And on days when he needed inspiration, he didn't have to look far.

"You still see Darren Oliver in the gym four, five days a week, and if he can get in there, I can get in there and the other guys can get in there too," Janssen says. "There was a day when I was dragging a little bit and [Mark] DeRosa came up to me and he's like, 'We're lifting.' And I said, 'All right.' Two days later, he was sitting at his locker, and I said, 'You got me, I'm gonna get you. We're going right now.'"

WAGNER, A ROOKIE AT age 29, came quickly to value the company of elders like Oliver and Janssen, who helped him learn what he calls "the graduate-level lessons." In the minors, scouting reports on opposing hitters evolve haphazardly, by word of mouth and personal experience. In the majors, sophisticated scouting reports and pervasive video constantly break down the strengths and weaknesses of hitters and pitchers alike. "Everything you do is exposed," Wagner says. So success requires study, as Janssen modelled for him, but it also requires trusting your own pitches. The balance is delicate.

"We were talking about a hit I gave up to a guy, and Oliver is like, 'You don't always have to over-think — you know, the scouting report said this or that,'" Wagner says. "If you focus on making a quality pitch, a lot of times you get outs because it's a good pitch. Darren offers a lot of sage wisdom about the game and how it's played."

In September, as Janssen turned 32 and wrapped up his first 30-save season, he said his shoulder was feeling "way better" than it had at any other time in 2013. The results reflected that. He saved games in each of his final 12 appearances, allowing only one run in that stretch. For the season, Janssen had 34 saves in 36 opportunities and posted a 2.56 ERA in 56 games.

The Blue Jays bullpen finished with the fourth-best ERA in the American League at 3.37, a remarkable feat given its relative inexperience, the staffing turnover, and a workload that covered 38 percent of the team's 1,452 innings pitched. Entering the season, the bullpen was a question mark. By the end, it was a strength, with sufficient depth for Alex Anthopoulos to muse that he might trade a reliever or two in a bid to shore up the rotation. But given the injuries that hampered Delabar and Cecil late in 2013, and the volatility of performance so typical of relievers, another solid year from the bullpen is far from certain.

Janssen expects to maintain his remarkable effectiveness and pitch with no worries about his shoulder in 2014. To that end, he planned to adopt a customized version of Delabar's weighted-ball regimen in the off-season. The program is designed to strengthen every part of the shoulder, including the decelerator muscles, responsible for braking the arm's forward motion, which some programs neglect. And if history holds, his fastball velocity should return. "I'm telling myself that," Janssen says. "There's a part of me that thinks there's still some more velocity in there."

And he will hope to play for a contender again. But as he looks around the clubhouse, he knows some of his teammates, and some of his bullpen mates too, will not be back. He knows that Anthopoulos cannot stand pat. "I wouldn't be extremely, extremely comfortable with the same roster next year," Janssen says. "Going forward, I'm sure there's got to be some changes here or there to get this thing right."

He hopes to stick around and be part of that solution. But after spending his whole career in one place, and using all of his physical and intellectual talents to make himself a proficient closer, one thing has come to matter more than anything else.

"I want to win," he says. "I want to win bad."

17 | THE EPIDEMIC

THE INVENTORY OF TORONTO Blue Jays body parts claimed by the meat grinder that is baseball's 162-game schedule went like this: an eye, a head, a hip, a lat, a wrist, two knees, two triceps, two forearms, three ankles, three shoulders, four obliques, and six elbows. That list does not include the tumour that grew in Melky Cabrera's lower spine, squeezing the nerves that feed his lower extremities. At season's end, their roster had recorded more ailments than an *Operation* board game. They had lost 1,380 player-games to injury, the most in the major leagues. Their 27 stints on the disabled list were second only to the New York Yankees, who had 28. Though baseball protocol is clear — never use injuries as an excuse for deficient performance, every team must cope with them, and the good ones overcome such obstacles — the Jays' attrition rate bordered on freakish.

It wasn't only the volume of injuries that bewildered the Blue Jays, but also the bizarre way so many of them went down. Brett Lawrie pulled an oblique diving harmlessly for a ball while playing for Canada in an exhibition game ahead of the World Baseball Classic. Jose Reyes, one of the best base-runners in the game, ripped up his ankle on one of the year's most awkward slides. J.A. Happ was struck in the head by a line drive and suffered a sprained right knee as he fell. Cabrera was shut down by knee problems and ended up having a tumour the size of a walnut removed from inside his spine. Edwin Encarnacion rolled over his left wrist on a slide and ended up needing surgery to repair torn cartilage. Colby Rasmus suffered a contusion on his left eye while trotting out to his position in centre field between innings, when he didn't see a routine warm-up throw coming from right-fielder Anthony Gose. "I know all guys go through injuries," Mark Buehrle lamented in August, "but this is starting to get a little ridiculous."

Lawrie's initial oblique injury occurred so innocently that he couldn't even pinpoint when it happened. That may have been an omen of the misery to come.

How strange did things get?

Well, consider the unusual chain of split-second events that led to the year's most pivotal injury, Reyes's sprained left ankle on April 12. Running on an 0-2 pitch with two outs and Cabrera batting, "I got confused," says Reyes, who since his first ankle injury in 2003 has always slid headfirst. "I thought Melky struck out and the inning was over. I had a great jump there, but I looked back to home plate a little bit late. When I picked up the catcher, I thought Melky struck out in my mind, and I saw the catcher throwing the ball to second base. I said, 'Oh man, what's going on here?' When I looked forward, the base was a couple of steps from me. I couldn't go headfirst because the base was so close. Everything happened so quick. I went feet first and that's when my cleat caught in the ground."

Reyes immediately clutched at his ankle, tried to get up, and then collapsed. Help came quickly. Trainer George Poulis asked him to move his ankle. He couldn't. He cried. "A lot of stuff went through my mind when he told me, 'Try to move your ankle' and I couldn't move my ankle," says Reyes. "In my mind, I thought the worst. 'Oh man, I broke this leg, I'm not going to play baseball again this year.' I knew that thing was serious . . . A lot of people asked me the question, 'What's going on, why are you sliding feet first? We've never seen you slide like that.' That was a terrible slide."

As terrible as that was, the sight of Happ being struck in the head by a Desmond Jennings line drive on May 7 was far more frightening.

Those who were at Tropicana Field that night can't forget the sickening pop the ball made when it smacked Happ on the skull behind the left ear. "By the loudness of the sound, I got pretty scared for him," said Jose Bautista. The tall left-hander collapsed in a heap. Players on both teams were badly shaken. "I just started praying on the spot," said R.A. Dickey. "That's all I knew to do." Yet Happ was out of hospital some 15 hours later, his right knee causing him far more difficulty than the pain in his head. He never once showed even the slightest symptoms of a concussion, but the sprain he suffered as he crumpled to the ground would keep him out until August. Happ's thoughts when he saw the replay? "I thought I made a decent pitch," he said with a smile. "I was frustrated."

That's certainly what the Blue Jays and Cabrera were feeling over the left fielder's perpetually-aching legs, which began to deteriorate during spring training and kept getting worse. By May his mobility had eroded badly — the team initially described his problems as irritation in his quads and hamstrings after an MRI found nothing substantial — and by the time he was placed on the DL for the first time at the end of June, he ran like a man with cinderblocks on his feet. He returned July 21 and played 10 games before he was shut down for good, tendinitis in his knees diagnosed as the culprit. But for four months Cabrera had been hiding back pain from the team, too, simply playing through it. "He was in extreme pain and couldn't sleep," said one person close to Cabrera. "He was so determined to repay the faith the organization had in him that he never wanted to come off the field." (On a June afternoon in the visitors' clubhouse at Tropicana Field, Cabrera stood patiently while Munenori Kawasaki plastered his back with coin-shaped therapeutic magnets, a device of debatable efficacy, but Cabrera was clearly willing to try anything.) Eventually, as he went through his rehabilitation work at the club's complex in Dunedin toward the end of August, the discomfort became too much to bear. An MRI revealed the tumour and it was promptly removed and found to be benign. Doctors told the Blue Jays the tumour surely impacted Cabrera's legs, and the initial prognosis was for a full recovery. "Now we have an explanation," said Anthopoulos. "A pretty serious one, but we do have an explanation for it."

As strange, not to mention worrying, as that was, nothing was more bizarre than the eye bruise Rasmus suffered as he headed to his position in the bottom of the first inning at Fenway Park on September 20. Gose, the right fielder, saw his teammate reach the edge of the outfield grass, thought he saw a signal, and fired a ball over for Rasmus and Rajai Davis to use during warm-ups. But Rasmus never saw it coming. It caught him flush on the eye, and soon he was in a local hospital getting tests. There was no major damage to his eyeball or orbital bone, but swelling and blurred vision meant his season was over. "I was just trying to get him the ball to play catch with Rajai," said an emotional Gose, "and I hit him in the face." Asked if he'd ever seen something similar, John Gibbons thought for a moment and replied, "No, no, no, I haven't."

And few had witnessed a team endure consecutive seasons with as many injuries as the Blue Jays. In 2012, they had 18 stints on the disabled list and 1,278 player-games lost to injury, fifth most in the majors, a phenomenon largely viewed as a fluke representing no cause for excessive concern. When even more injuries piled up in 2013, Anthopoulos said he was determined to get to the bottom of it. "I think we have to," he said. "Normally you can say it's one year, it may have been an anomaly, but there are certain types of injuries that we need to look at, and why they're happening. It's not always an easy thing to explain, but there's no doubt. That's why depth is so important, but at the same time, injury prevention is more important than depth. Definitely something we're going to talk about." And as they consider trades and free agents in the future, the Jays will be more circumspect when examining a player's medical history. "We may have to manage our risk a little bit more, and not be as willing to take on as much risk from a medical standpoint," Anthopoulos said.

On the Friday of the final weekend of the season, Lawrie was struck in the face by a pitch from Tampa Bay's Roberto Hernandez. It was a frightening moment, and Lawrie left the game bleeding from his mouth. But the next day, sporting a fat lip but no stitches and surprised that his teeth were all in place, Lawrie was back in the lineup. Hernandez had thrown an 83-mph changeup instead of his 91-mph fastball. Lawrie had turned his head just enough to deflect the ball and dodge a debilitating impact. For once in this season of medical misery, a Blue Jays injury looked worse than it was.

| 18 | ASSESSING THE DAMAGE |

PLAYER EVALUATION IS A fickle, error-prone business, one in which even the best and brightest front offices function in the realm of educated guesswork. They tend to be wrong more often than right. Admittedly, the rise of stats-based scouting and new-age metrics, combined with the pervasiveness of video, have advanced the field, but the process will never be foolproof. Every once in a while a team still needs a dose of luck. And did the Blue Jays ever get lucky with Edwin Encarnacion, undoubtedly their best player in 2013 (and 2012, too, for that matter).

Absurd as it seems now, back when he was acquired from the Cincinnati Reds on July 31, 2009, as part of the Scott Rolen deal, the Blue Jays didn't want him *at all*. In fact, the man cruelly dubbed E5 in Cincy because of dodgy play in the field was forced upon them, the price they had to pay in order to acquire Zach Stewart, then a top prospect, and Josh Roenicke, a promising reliever at the time. Twice in the next year and a half they dumped Encarnacion, first outrighting him to Triple-A Las Vegas on June 21, 2010, and later placing him on waivers during the off-season. The second time, the Oakland Athletics claimed him and spent three weeks choosing between him and fellow third baseman Kevin Kouzmanoff, eventually cutting Encarnacion loose again. On December 16, with no other takers, he re-signed with the Blue Jays, and when he slumped badly out of the gate in 2011, John Farrell advocated for his release. Instead, Alex Anthopoulos opted to drop Juan Rivera. Eventually, Encarnacion locked into a new approach at the plate, adopted a two-handed finish to his swing before the 2012 season, and blossomed into a star. Meanwhile, the guys the Blue Jays *really* wanted from the Reds, Stewart (who was used to help land Colby Rasmus in July 2011) and Roenicke, became fringe major-leaguers bouncing from organization to organization. Rarely does being wrong work out so well.

As September 2013 arrived and their season moved drearily toward its conclusion, there was no happy ending to ease the sting of just how wrong the Blue Jays' assessments were in the previous off-season. Even though a run of 10 wins in 13 contests — their most successful stretch since June's 11-game win streak — provided a refreshing respite from the summer gloom, the roster's many flaws were laid bare on the field, while some players privately questioned the clubhouse dynamic. It was difficult to determine how much of the latter was legitimate, and how much was simply the natural by-product of the accumulated frustration generated by losing. "When you lose a lot more games than you expected," J.A. Happ says, "it starts wearing on you and you start noticing things that you normally wouldn't notice when you're winning." Either way, things were a mess.

Encarnacion was among the few exceptions, his transformation into Steady Eddie continuing unabated amid the troubles around him. Questions about whether he'd be able to repeat his 2012 breakout were answered in July with the first all-star selection of his career. On September 2 his home run in a 4-1 win over the Arizona Diamondbacks made him just the fourth player in Blue Jays history to post consecutive seasons of at least 35 homers and 100 RBIs. That production, combined with his steely, unflappable demeanour, gradually elevated him into one of the team's most important leaders. Despite not being the rah-rah type, he was viewed as someone his teammates would follow. "I just tried to be the same guy I've been all my career," he says of growing into a leadership role. "I'm very quiet. I know I had a couple of good years and that's made everybody look at me now, look at what I do, but I've kept doing the same [things] I've been doing all my career, so I don't have to change anything. That's me."

There was certainly no need for Encarnacion to change. He finished with 36 homers, tied for third in the majors, as well as 104 RBIs and a .904 OPS in 142 games. (His season was cut short by surgery to repair torn cartilage in his left wrist.) But neither his monster numbers nor the club's strong run could divert attention from the ongoing post-mortem on 2013's train wreck. Everyone from Anthopoulos and his staff to the casual fan had a theory on why the ride to the post-season had derailed so badly. The GM's pledge that John Gibbons would return as manager quieted one of the primary talking points, but did little to inspire confidence among the fan base.

The other obvious issue for critics to pick at was a starting rotation that finished 29th in the majors with a 4.81 ERA, a harsh fact that Anthopoulos repeatedly raised in interviews. And certainly a better rotation would have turned the club's fate dramatically. "We need the pitchers to do their job," Encarnacion says. "When they do good, we win games. Everywhere it's the same. When you have good pitching you're going to win . . . We've got to keep everything together. When we had that 11-game winning streak, we kept everything together, the pitching and the offence, and we were winning. After that, we didn't hit, the pitching staff didn't do their work — we're not going to win like that."

But the issues ran deeper and required more than a couple of tweaks to the starting staff to fix. Put simply, the Blue Jays were just too loose in too many facets of the game — batters not moving runners over, infielders failing to turn double plays, pitchers nibbling at the edges of the plate instead of attacking hitters — and the extra pitches and free outs they gave their opponents cost them. Combined with a patchwork starting rotation adept at building deficits fast and making exits early, the Jays' troubles in the margins became lethal, eroding their dazzling collection of talent from the inside. The Blue Jays were like a house built with the finest bricks and the cheapest mortar. "In the [American League East] you can't give opportunities to the other teams because every team in our division is very good," says Jose Reyes. "You need to find a way to win the tough games. I feel like we have a lot of games we should have won. We didn't do that, and that cost us. We made some mistakes, and we need to learn for next year, because when you're making too many mistakes in this game, it's going to cost you. And you can see it in the way we played this year. We're in last place. That's not good to say because our expectations were so high at the beginning of the season. To be here now, in September, in last place, it's disappointing because we have unbelievable talent in this clubhouse, and we weren't able to do anything."

NO OPPONENT HURT THE Blue Jays as much during the 2013 season as the New York Yankees, who won 14 of the 19 meetings between the clubs, even after dropping two of three during a mid-September series in Toronto. That the Bronx Bombers managed to stay in contention until the final week of the season despite the lengthy injury absences of such key pieces as Derek Jeter, Mark Teixeira, Alex Rodriguez, Kevin Youkilis, Curtis Granderson, Michael Pineda, and Francisco Cervelli was nothing short of remarkable. Consider, too, that they had to deal with the ongoing circus surrounding Rodriguez's 211-game doping suspension and appeal, and that they patched up their roster holes by bottom feeding on a series of reclamation projects. The Yankees were a perfect study in contrast to the Blue Jays.

How did they do it? "There's outside expectation and there's what we have in the clubhouse," says Vernon Wells, the former Blue Jays outfielder dealt to the Yankees in March by the Los Angeles Angels. "[General manager Brian] Cashman brought in a bunch of veteran guys who have been around the block and seen a lot of different things and asked us to do what we can, not try to shoulder things, not try to replace who isn't there, because you can't replace what's missing. Just go out and be a complete lineup." That's exactly what they did, wringing whatever they could from the likes of Wells, Travis Hafner, Lyle Overbay, and Jayson Nix, mixing steady and crisp baseball with league-average pitching. They played up to their environment and became a greater whole. "It's because of the tradition that comes with [playing for the Yankees]," says Wells. "When you talk about an organization that won 27 championships, and is as thirsty for 28 as a team that doesn't have any, that's what it's all about, and it's about doing your part to help this team win. That's all that's talked about."

The Blue Jays, on the other hand, were collectively a far lesser whole. While the spate of injuries that exposed a lack of depth, particularly in the rotation, played a significant role, so too did poor fundamentals, inconsistent execution, and what some players privately felt was an insufficient internal accountability.

In hindsight, the troubles may have started during the short work days at the beginning of spring training, when John Gibbons trusted his veteran players to do what they needed to be ready for the regular season. The practice is common for experienced clubs; it conserves energy and health for the looming marathon. Says bench coach DeMarlo Hale: "These guys have played baseball long enough. It's not like it's a rookie team. They're some veterans who have success and have track records." But for some Blue Jays, the defensive instincts typically locked down through tedious reps never seemed to become second nature, and as a result, occasional misplays popped up at inopportune times during the regular season.

"Maybe we got a little too much leeway than we deserved — maybe," says Mark DeRosa. "I think on paper we were as talented a team as could be coming into camp, so who's to fault Gibby for maybe giving us a little bit more leeway? It's not like we were a young club when we first broke camp. We were a veteran team. I mean, with Bobby Cox [in Atlanta] we went through pickoffs and relays once in spring, and if you had no chance of making the team and you whipped it into centre field, it wasn't like we were going to sit there for 15 minutes and go over it. 'You won't play in the big leagues *until* you can execute that, so I ain't gonna worry about it' . . . So we went through it really quick because we were so locked."

Further complicating matters early on was that Brett Lawrie's oblique injury during the spring forced Maicer Izturis to share time at third base with DeRosa, surrendering significant defensive range and ability. With Izturis occupied, Emilio Bonifacio carried the early load at second base. But often, he was baffled by how quickly balls came at him on the Rogers Centre's artificial turf. The Reyes injury 10 games into the season catapulted Munenori Kawasaki and his substandard range and arm into an everyday role. With two exceptional defenders on the shelf, makeable outs often became hits and double plays weren't turned. And a slumping offence meant pitchers had virtually no margin for error. The infield defence stabilized somewhat when Lawrie returned, but as Izturis settled in at second base, his limited range was again exposed. The stunning difference when sure-handed shortstop prospect Ryan Goins took over at second after his mid-August call-up only underlined how porous the defence had been up the middle. "You're definitely going to see us, going forward, making defence a priority in the infield," said Anthopoulos. "If you get a really special bat, there's always a tradeoff, but for the most part, we would definitely go defence first."

The play of Goins, a product of a farm system lambasted in the media and fan base for producing fundamentally flawed players, raised an interesting question. Was the Blue Jays' deficient play in the field more the result of poor preparation or poor personnel? Goins did all the same drills as Izturis and Bonifacio during spring training, so if the process was flawed he should have flopped, too. Yet seeing him play second base after five months of watching his predecessors made the 25-year-old seem like the second coming of Roberto Alomar. And in some ways, he was. A memorable example came in a 2-0 win September 8 at Minnesota, when the rookie made a game-changing defensive play in the sixth inning. With runners on the corners and none out in a 0-0 game, he fielded Chris Herrmann's grounder and, rather than conceding the run for a double play, threw home to get Pedro Florimon and preserve the tie. It was a play that most second basemen don't even attempt, let alone make. Izturis and Bonifacio would have been hard-pressed to simply turn two.

Third base coach Luis Rivera, who's in charge of the infielders, seemed perplexed by his club's work around the diamond. "We made a lot of careless errors," he says. "Sometimes you watch and there's an error over here, an error over there and [you] wonder how we continue to make those errors when these guys are good enough not to make them. Maybe it has to do with concentration, maybe it has to do with going in and out of AstroTurf, quick infields to slow infields. There might be a lot of things that are part of that."

At season's end, Anthopoulos readily admitted the Blue Jays front office needed to adjust the way it evaluated defenders to more heavily weigh the turf's effect on a player's skills. He also spoke of scheduling more spring training drills on the turf-covered half-diamond in Dunedin, even though that surface plays noticeably slower than the one in Toronto.

Anthopoulos also wondered whether the departure of eight players to the World Baseball Classic played a role. Edwin Encarnacion, Jose Reyes, and Moises Sierra joined the eventual champion Dominican Republic team, while Brett Lawrie, Trystan Magnuson, and Adam Loewen suited up for Canada, and R.A. Dickey and J.P. Arencibia represented the United States.

Factor everything together against the backdrop of expectations, and a collective series of small missteps and aberrations may have accumulated into a larger problem.

DeRosa stresses that the Jays defenders did all of the standard spring drills in Dunedin. But he adds, "I think if we could go back in time and do it, guys maybe would've got a little bit less leeway and we would have maybe covered fundamentals a little bit more, hit it harder."

Dickey, who missed three weeks of camp because of the Classic, agrees that Gibbons gave his veterans plenty of leeway in spring training. "When I was [in Dunedin], I felt like I had the latitude, the flexibility — and maybe that's part of what is the perception of the problem, that there was too much latitude and flexibility. But for an older guy who knows exactly what he needs to do to get his body ready, and you know he's not going to take advantage of that, it was great for me. Now, obviously, I think you're going to see a much different spring training next year. I think that's going to help us. I think we're probably going to see a few longer days, some more intensive work, especially infield play. I don't make out the spring training schedule, but I feel like that's coming and certainly will be welcomed by me."

THE BLUE JAYS EXTRACTED a small measure of satisfaction on September 19 by effectively ending the Yankees' hopes of sneaking into the post-season with a 6-2 victory, but there would be no killing the Red Sox's vibe during the three-game series at Fenway Park that followed.

Dramatically remade during the off-season to much less fanfare, John Farrell's crew became everything the Blue Jays were not, combining strong starting pitching with a relentless offence and sharp defence. Rarely did they let opponents breathe, building up a nine-game lead in the standings and rocking the best record in the American League at 93-61 when Toronto arrived in Boston. All they needed was a single victory to secure their first East division crown since 2007.

Foregone conclusion or not, the last thing the Blue Jays wanted to see was the Red Sox clinch right in front of them. The best-case scenario would have been for them to win and let a Tampa Bay loss hand Boston the title. But Toronto starter Esmil Rogers walked five batters in two and one-third innings and left the game trailing 2-0. After the Jays crept within one, Boston scored four late runs to seal a 6-3 win, triggering bedlam among the 37,215 gathered at the place pompously dubbed America's Most Beloved Ballpark. Koji Uehara — who used his no-trade clause to block a trade from Texas to Toronto before the 2012 season — closed it out in the ninth, striking out Brett Lawrie to end the game.

Waiting on deck was Adam Lind, the slugging first baseman–DH who chafed under Farrell the previous two seasons and had been publicly critical of his former manager. After strike three, Lind walked slowly from the on-deck circle to the Blue Jays dugout, taking quick peeks to his right at the Red Sox celebrating on the infield. He paused at the top step, turned back for one more look, then made his way down the stairs and into the clubhouse. Only a handful of Blue Jays, Lawrie among them, could stomach a longer glance.

Compounding the gloom were the familiar faces on the other side, notably Farrell and coaches Brian Butterfield and Torey Lovullo. "I spent a lot of time with their staff the last couple of years — one of the harder things I've witnessed in this game was watching that. I'm not real thrilled right now," Lind said. "Tough, tough loss, just in the fact of the history — you know everything. It somehow seems fitting the way it just worked out."

Butterfield, a third base coach with the Blue Jays for 10 and a half seasons, and Lovullo, a first base coach the previous two years, both left Toronto for Boston with Farrell. Butterfield beamed as he shared a celebratory beer in the dugout with pitcher John Lackey, while Lovullo chugged champagne on the field when joyous players weren't dousing him. Even the usually stone-faced Farrell cracked a smile, waving to a teeming throng of elated fans ringing the Red Sox dugout as they chanted his name, and raising his arm as he stepped into NESN's makeshift on-field set for a TV interview. It was another stinging insult for the Blue Jays, and for some this one cut deeper. Yet given the chance to gloat, the man so reviled in Toronto declined. "You go into the situation knowing that you try to take advantage of the strengths of your team, but it became very clear in spring training that we felt like we had a special group, and it's been able to play out," he says when asked if this was the type of scene that made managing the Red Sox his dream job. "Baseball is very much the fabric of Boston and our market. It's evident every night we play in here. Our guys love the environment, the energy that's created in here, and we've been able to thrive on it."

As unpalatable as the scene was for the Blue Jays and their fans, it was impossible not to have at least a grudging respect for all the Red Sox accomplished, and the way they played after going 69-93 in 2012. They didn't lose more than three games in a row during the regular season en route to a 97-65 finish, and save for a 2-9 stretch May 3–14, were remarkably steady. Right after their down period, they responded with five consecutive victories, and wins in 10 of their next 13 outings. There was never any let-up. "We got players from winning environments," says Farrell. "They understand not only the game but that it takes a group. It's not a game of individuals, it's one unit. In spring training, we made it very clear that we wanted to make the daily focal point the game that night, not anything else that goes on around it. To me, that's somewhat the beacon that lets everything else fall in line. Our preparation, the individual routines, led up to the game that night, and how we work inside it to hopefully take home a win."

While the Red Sox basked in the moment outside, the Blue Jays were ensconced in the cramped and decrepit visitor's clubhouse, silently dodging laundry carts and teammates navigating the narrow pathways. In his office, John Gibbons spoke admiringly of Boston's tenacity. So too did Mark DeRosa, who saw opportunity where others saw bitterness. "I look at it as motivation," he says. "I look at it as the best team won. Start to finish they were the best team in our division, and to win the AL East with the talent that's in this division is something to be proud of. They got high character guys. Not only that, they got guys who really care about putting team first, and they found a way. It's nice when you have [Jon] Lester, [Clay] Buchholz, and those [other starters] they run out there, too. You've got to perform, but at the same time, they were the best team, I felt."

Left unsaid was that the Blue Jays were not a team in the way the Red Sox were. That's not surprising, given how much baggage had accumulated by then. There was the slow start in April, the unsteady recovery in May, the return of hope in June, and the subsequent crash in July and August. And with the drama playing out before a newly engaged fan base and intensive media coverage, there was nowhere to hide, and so much to lament, especially the 7-19 stretch that followed the 11-game win streak. Five of those losses were by one run, two more were by two runs, and another came in extra innings. The Jays often fell short by a hit, a pitch, or a defensive play.

"That was a big point of our season," says Casey Janssen. "We got off to a slow start, we were in catch-up mode right out of the gate. You look back now and you're like, dang, those were two big stretches that put us behind the eight ball. You work so hard for that 11-game win streak, then you have a loss, no big deal, but then you go on a tough stretch. It's like everyone starts to exhale and you can only whip your horse so many times before it just doesn't have anything . . . As those teams distanced themselves from us, it just made it tougher and tougher. Not only are we trying to catch them, but we're running out of games and we're not playing good against the teams ahead of us."

In that context, two comments made by Los Angeles Dodgers manager Don Mattingly resonated. Off to a slow start despite carrying baseball's biggest payroll, the Dodgers arrived at their low point with a loss at San Diego on June 21, falling to 30-42. Two days later, the Blue Jays hit their high-water mark at 38-36 after an 11th straight win. From then on, the fates of both clubs reversed. Mattingly remembers noticing the Blue Jays' surge and thinking, "There were some parallels for our club," and once the Dodgers turned things around, "we wanted to make sure at that point to keep momentum. If you let it get away, it goes the other direction."

The other comment worth noting — largely because some in the Blue Jays clubhouse shared the same sentiment — came May 22, as Mattingly discussed the Dodgers' early struggles. "Part of it is your mixture of competitiveness, too," he said that day. "It's not just, 'Let's go put an all-star team out there, and play games, and the team with the all-star team wins.' It's trying to find that balance of a team that's got a little grit, and a little fight. They'll fight you and have enough talent to get there also, with that. All grit and no talent is not going to get you there, and all talent and no grit is not going to get you there. There's got to be a mixture of both."

The Blue Jays were swept by Mattingly's team in July in Toronto, but they should have won two of the three games, blowing late leads in both. The Dodgers went on to win the National League West with a 92-70 record thanks not only to their overwhelming talent, but the determined way they played. In a noticeable shift on the final day of the regular season, Alex Anthopoulos sounded more willing than he's ever been to look beyond a player's tools. "You always try to balance it out," he said. "There are definitely scenarios where on the production side you'll take a little less to get some of the other things that players bring. That being said, if we can do that we certainly will, but the focus will be on the rotation. It needs to be."

ONE OF THE LAZIEST and most clichéd narratives in sports is that of The Leader. Yes, there are some athletes who are natural-born unifiers, able to inspire disparate personalities to focus on a single goal and deliver the inspirational speeches that saccharine Hollywood movies are made of. Players like that are rarities. That's why Derek Jeter, Dustin Pedroia, Buster Posey, and their ilk, players who come to embody a franchise's persona, are so special. Often the best clubs have multiple leaders who go about their business in different ways, and usually, it's what a player does on the field that matters most. But when a team struggles, it's convenient for critics to point to a lack of leadership, although the fault typically lies in a collective failure. Yet there's also an element of accountability that players with strong leadership qualities bring to a ball club. And without a player, or more ideally a group of players, willing to accept and demand responsibility, an environment that feels free of consequence can develop.

The role of the Blue Jays' clubhouse leadership became a debating topic in early September, with Jose Bautista again becoming a target. A fresh round of chatter about whether the Blue Jays should trade their star slugger arose after injury again cut his season short. This time it was a bone bruise atop his femur suffered while pulling up as he crossed the plate in August. Regurgitating the same arguments from April, fans criticized him for failing to be a good leader, setting a poor example, and being selfish. The latter reproach stemmed largely from two high-profile late-game ejections resulting from his anger over called strikes in June and July. When the focus needed to be on winning games, he gave into his frustrations and vented at umpires rather than locking in on the next pitch. Some fans concluded that the all-star right fielder had become part of the problem, rather than part of the solution, a notion sanctioned by Jerry Howarth, the Blue Jays' radio announcer of 32 years.

During pre-season play, Howarth censured Bautista publicly for arguing with umpires and failing to run out a ground ball, and on October 2 made even more pointed comments on the club's flagship station, Sportsnet 590 The Fan. Responding to a question from host Jeff Blair, Howarth said Bautista, once a respected leader, had become a poor role model for his teammates. "That negative attitude [was evident] especially with umpires, and his continual complaining, and giving up at-bats," he said. "And one time, with a runner at first base and one out, hitting a fly ball to right field, and he turned and walked back to the third base dugout. What is going on here? Here's what happened: Jose Reyes, a good kid, a four-time all-star, he started to complain about the umpiring, because of who? Jose Bautista. When Bautista wasn't there, the last month and a half, that allowed Jose Reyes and Edwin Encarnacion to emerge as leaders. That's what you want in 2014. And if Bautista can give you something, a piece that you don't have right now, do it, because the other leaders are in place, and all they need is that opening to take and run with it, and I can see them doing that."

The stunningly harsh commentary from the usually genial Howarth demonstrated how far the outlook on Bautista had turned, not only within the fan base, but also among some around the team. The time was ripe for griping after all, and several did so privately drawing similar conclusions to Howarth. For the record, Reyes, who rarely argued with umpires during his injury-interrupted season, was ejected from one game. After a called third strike, he threw his helmet in anger (grounds for automatic ejection) on August 22, two days after Bautista's final game, and had no further noticeable disputes with umpires after that. And unlike the end of 2012, when he left the team following wrist surgery, Bautista stayed until the last week of the season, sitting on the bench with his teammates during games.

The discussion over Bautista's perceived shortcomings as a leader often ignored his quantifiable contributions, which were significant. Among qualified American League batters, he ranked in the top 12 in home runs (28), slugging percentage (.498), on-base plus slugging (.856), and walk percentage (13.1). Any possible fluctuation in the quality of his work as a leader was, of course, impossible to measure, as well as what impact, if any, that would have had on the team. As for Bautista, he insists it wasn't a lack of leadership that sabotaged the Blue Jays in 2013. "There's different types of leadership from different types of people, they're all needed, they're all warranted, but it's not like you can't survive or cannot be successful without them," he says. "It doesn't rest solely on one person. Everybody to a certain degree is a leader. I just hope people don't try to use it as an excuse for the lack of success we've had this year, that there's been a lack of leadership here. I don't believe that's the case, and I don't believe that's why we haven't won the games we were supposed to win this year."

Asked to define his view of his leadership role, he replies, "It's hard for me to analyze it in that perspective. First and foremost, I have to make sure I'm helping the team win games, and keeping myself having enough drive so that I can compete to the best of my abilities. After that, it's setting a good example for the rest of the guys in here, especially the young guys, by the way I conduct myself on and off the field, the way I prepare for games, and the way I play the game. That's pretty much it. I don't necessarily have to go out of my way too much to do stuff because it's been appointed to me that I'm the leader, or call team meetings every week. That's not what a leader does. I hope people don't think that's what I'm supposed to do, or that any other person that's a leader on this team is supposed to do."

Unless it's needed, and at times it was. Bautista was there with Mark DeRosa to bring the players together for their first team meeting at the end of April, and it was he, DeRosa, Edwin Encarnacion, Melky Cabrera, and Adam Lind who met with John Gibbons after the five-error debacle against the Dodgers on July 22, advising the manager of their plans to hold a players-only meeting the next day.

Still, a sense around the team is that more vocal leadership from someone who played every day would help. Like DeRosa, a part-time player, pitchers Mark Buehrle and Darren Oliver provided well-respected veteran voices, but throughout baseball it is generally accepted that only an everyday player can take aside another everyday player to demand more. Some felt Jose Reyes could grow into that role, but he was new to the Blue Jays and missed nearly half of the season with the ankle injury. Coming back and suddenly asserting his leadership wouldn't have played well. Due to his quiet nature, Encarnacion was more of a lead-by-example type, as were Lind and Colby Rasmus.

"Leadership can always be better," says Casey Janssen. "I feel like a young person can lead just as much as a veteran, and I still think we need that leader that plays the game the right way every single day and is one of the guys that isn't afraid to get in somebody's face . . . It's somebody who says, 'Hey, this isn't how it's done, or this isn't how we go about things, or off the field act professional, run balls out hard every single time, don't take plays off.' Stuff like that. I don't think we've had that Pedroia-type guy who fights for everything he does and commands so much respect everywhere he is. Pedroia is not the biggest guy in the league, but his role on his team is as big as anyone's."

While at the time Alex Anthopoulos praised the July team meeting as an example of internal accountability and players resolving problems amongst themselves, rarely are such gatherings a good sign. Teams don't hold players-only meetings unless troublesome issues need resolution. "Those were more like the boiling-point type meetings," says Janssen, "as opposed to seeing it right on the spot and addressing it right on the spot and not letting it get to that point. Not giving someone a free pass, and doing it right there. If it's not running a ball out hard, or not getting a bunt down, not getting to first base on a [pitcher's fielding] play or something like that — 'Hey, that can't happen.' The person probably knows, but if you hear it more times, you're going to get better and hopefully figure it out, and find a way to make it work. You've got to all be pulling from the same rope, and if guys aren't willing to be a quote-unquote *team*, you start going in different directions."

The coaching staff can only deliver that message so often. As Gibbons, speaking in general terms, pointed out from time to time, if players can't settle such matters among themselves, a team is sunk, especially once the inevitable adversity inherent in the 162-game grind strikes. Adds Mark Buehrle, "When you're winning, everything is taking care of itself and everything is good, and when you're losing, everything gets magnified. I don't think we did anything different from when we were on the 11-game win streak to when we lost 10 out of 11, or whatever it is. It's the way we play on the field. When we suck, we suck. I don't know that it came down to leadership. Everybody needed to step up and play to their capabilities."

Bautista echoes those sentiments, taking responsibility for his play first and foremost and not pointing a finger elsewhere. He also insists he's the same player he's always been, and that since his breakout in 2010, he doesn't think he has needed "to go above and beyond and do more. But I think there's less stuff you can get away with because you have to watch yourself more . . . To me it hasn't made that much of a difference. But I do get criticized and scrutinized more now for the some of the same things I did before that nobody cared about. Now it's a big deal."

As for what went wrong in 2013, Bautista points to the obvious: the impact of injuries and lack of performance. "I have to mention my name first because I've had a decent year but I don't feel like I've been as consistent as I should have been and that I've had as good a year as I should have had," he says. "With the opportunities these guys gave me in front of me getting on base, I feel like I should have a ton more RBIs, and that I should have been putting the ball in play more consistently. That's just not acceptable to me. There have been plenty of games where we've been one key hit away at one particular moment where we could have won the game. Every team can go back and say the same thing, but it's happened to us more than it does a normal team. It's like the one little mistake we might make in a particular game costs us the game."

Leadership alone won't fix that. Nor will a different spring singularly make everything better. Nor will improved fundamentals or a different clubhouse culture fix all. There's no simple panacea. But with collective gains made in each of those areas, maybe some of the games that were lost in the margins would have turned out differently. There's no debating how much a better rotation would have changed the 2013 season for the Blue Jays, but quality starters in isolation wouldn't have patched all the other cracks in the mortar. In mid-September, as the Cleveland Indians surged toward the post-season, Nick Swisher cited some words of wisdom from his manager, Terry (Tito) Francona, that stuck with him. "It's like Tito told us in spring training," Swisher said. "'Bad teams pick each other apart, good teams pick each other up.'" How much of the former the Blue Jays did is debatable, but they certainly didn't do enough of the latter.

SALACIOUS CONTROVERSY FOLLOWED THE Red Sox's colossal collapse in September 2011, when they blew a nine-game lead and missed the playoffs. The narrative most fans remember featured several starting pitchers eating fried chicken, drinking beer, and playing video games in the clubhouse during games down the stretch. Often lost, however, is that the Red Sox simply ran out of healthy pitching. The team had internal issues, to be sure, but good health and talent can overcome a lot.

That's why simple randomness can't be overlooked when examining the Blue Jays' struggles, as well. The natural inclination is to engage in extensive navel-gazing and identify root-cause problems, but sometimes there's nothing more to it than chance. "Toronto could have won the division by six, eight, 10 games if their pitchers were healthy and it came together," says Matt Sosnick, the agent for Josh Johnson. "Every move Alex made was weighted in his favour. It just didn't work out. He played the percentages perfectly . . . The team on the field is good enough to win a World Series. Guys just have to stay healthy and perform."

As much as everyone wanted answers, maybe the whole mess, all the injuries and disappointment, was born out of little more than bad luck. Maybe winning just wasn't meant to be. "There's more to winning than just the one-on-one competition," says John Gibbons. "You're with each other for six or seven months in a row. Sometimes there can be tension, and sometimes everybody's not on the same page. Sometimes you bring a lot of guys together and it doesn't fit, or it takes awhile to fit. That's just the way it is. Even if you have guys that have been around awhile, sometimes [it takes time to] gel. Sometimes it never happens. Nobody knows for sure if that's the reason a team struggles."

That's the thing; no one can say for certain why, in a given year, a collection of good players does not make a good team. Just as the Blue Jays couldn't have predicted Edwin Encarnacion's sudden ascent from salary dump to thriving star, there's no sure-fire blueprint for guaranteeing a winner.

All any general manager can do is try to accumulate as much talent as possible, try to create a positive environment for his team to succeed in, and hire a manager who fits his vision along with competent coaches to extract the best out of everyone. That's exactly what Alex Anthopoulos did before the 2013 season. For a myriad of reasons it blew up in his face, and for the 20th straight year, all the Blue Jays and their fans were left with was a tired refrain: there's always next year.

EPILOGUE

TWENTY MINUTES AFTER THE Blue Jays finished their season with a 7-6 loss to Tampa Bay and a 74-88 record, their clubhouse was already half-empty, with a handful of players still packing up their lockers, surrounded by stalls that were barren save for dangling hangers. Jose Reyes, still clad in his Captain America undershirt, sat in one corner of the clubhouse, sending text messages and stuffing a duffel bag. Casey Janssen tossed old cleats into a box of used items to be donated. Brett Lawrie gave Anthony Gose a hug and told him to text over the winter. Munenori Kawasaki, as always, bounced around, showing off his rapidly improving English in creative ways. Darren Oliver, wearing a trendy zip-up, shook a few hands as he walked out of a big-league clubhouse for the final time as a player.

This wasn't how it was supposed to end. Game number 162 was supposed to have meaning, cresting with exuberant players popping champagne. The season finale did have meaning — for the Rays, who nearly blew a 7-0 lead but held on to clinch a tie for a wild-card berth with the Texas Rangers. The next night in Arlington, they beat the Rangers and advanced to the post-season. As they were in Boston a couple of weeks earlier, the Blue Jays were reluctant contributors to a rival's celebration.

"If I could take one adjective to describe the season for me, I think it would be *sad*," says R.A. Dickey, "simply because I feel like at times we really showed flashes of being who we were made to be as a team in the off-season. A lot of different things played into that — injuries, a lot of different individual personalities being thrown into the mix all at once without having a chance to really [gel]. But I think I'm sad because I felt when I signed my extension here for three years we were going to have a credible shot to win the AL East, and one of those three years has now passed us by. I'm sad because I think we've shown flashes of what we can be, and it gets you all excited. An 11-game win streak — I've never been part of an 11-game win streak. That was pretty awesome. And I felt like we gave the fans and the masses a glimpse of what we could be. We just couldn't carry it out. That's sad to me."

Even amid the sadness, there were some positives in 2013. Attendance at Rogers Centre surged dramatically to 2,536,562, an increase of 436,899 over 2012, and the Blue Jays' best total since 1997. That settled any lingering doubts about how the people of Toronto would respond to a team of promise. Edwin Encarnacion took a significant step into the ranks of the game's elite hitters. Brett Lawrie started to mature. Dickey and Buehrle became the first Blue Jays pitching duo to each break the 200-inning plateau since Roy Halladay and A.J. Burnett in 2008. Kyle Drabek and Drew Hutchison both completed their rehabilitation from Tommy John surgery and made major progress toward regaining their form. Combined with knocking-on-the-door prospects Sean Nolin and Marcus Stroman, the Blue Jays should have far more promising alternatives waiting in the wings at Triple-A Buffalo should the 2014 rotation falter. And two beleaguered hitters, Adam Lind and Colby Rasmus, showed signs of growth and renewed prosperity.

Lind had never come close to matching his breakout season of 2009, and finally, he began to understand why. "I wasn't being a smart hitter," he said. "I was being stubborn and, for lack of a better word, stupid." In 2013, he began to focus on hitting the pitches he wanted in the locations he preferred, rather than swinging at everything. He improved his strike-zone discipline, drawing 51 walks, almost as many as he had taken in his previous two seasons combined. "You've got to learn to take [certain pitches]," he says. "Pitchers here put their pitches in a better spot, and their pitches have more bite, more depth, more velocity. It might feel like you're cheating in a way. That's why some young hitters don't want to [take pitches], because it feels like cheating. Really, it's being a smart hitter. You're going to take some fastballs right down the middle, but over the course of 162 games, the product will be better." It was for Lind. Finishing with a blistering September (.346 average, seven homers, 20 RBIs), he enjoyed his best season since 2009, batting .288 with 23 homers and an .854 OPS. He also stayed off the disabled list, despite occasional recurrences of the back spasms that sidelined him in 2011 and 2012.

Since coming from St. Louis in a 2011 trade, Rasmus was a troubled soul and an erratic hitter who showed flashes of prodigious power. Once a can't-miss prospect, his confidence sagged in the high-pressure environment created by former Cardinals manager Tony La Russa. "I just try to play hard and have fun," Rasmus says. "But La Russa didn't like that answer. He's like, 'This ain't fun, we're trying to win.' And to me, it never made sense. All the people in St. Louis were like, 'You should be doing this, you should be hitting .300 with 30 [homers] every year.'" The criticism stung him deeply. "I never could let it go," he says. "When I'd get home, in the morning I'd wake up and the mailman would come at me and say, 'You need to be hitting the ball the other way.'"

Rasmus finally started to let it go in 2013. He developed an easy rapport with Gibbons and hitting coach Chad Mottola. To keep his body strong and his mind clear, he curbed his habit of overworking in the batting cage after a bad game. He batted .276 with 22 homers and an .840 OPS. His 4.8 WAR (wins above replacement) ranked third — behind Mike Trout and Jacoby Ellsbury — among American League centre fielders with 450 or more plate appearances. "I'm definitely better," Rasmus says. "I still got some demons in my head I'm trying to get out, but that's just part of it, part of things that scar you along the way."

By July, he was saying he would no longer talk about the scars of St. Louis when reporters came calling. It was time to stop looking over his shoulder. "I'm not about bashing anybody," he says. "I'm not trying to get that in the paper and having them read it, because that's not what I'm about."

In the context of an 88-loss season, however, there was little consolation in the good work of individual players. Those silver linings amid the post-mortems only emphasized how poorly the striking off-season moves, previously hailed as pure genius, played out for Alex Anthopoulos. Some debated whether the wunderkind GM, having swung for the fences and missed so badly, miscalculated the timing of his team's big jump forward. He knew the club lacked starting depth and wondered in hindsight if it was an ill-conceived risk to count on Dickey, Buehrle, Brandon Morrow, Josh Johnson, J.A. Happ, and Ricky Romero to be healthy and effective enough to carry the load.

What he didn't second guess was the decision to go all-in, to open the competitive window when he did. Fans frustrated by the outcome in 2013 might not have been much happier with the alternative.

The Blue Jays "were going to go in one of two directions [after the 2012 season] — just being in the middle is the wrong way to go," says Anthopoulos. "Are we going to trade everybody away and continue on the completely young path? Hechavarria, Marisnick, Gose, Syndergaard, Nicolino, Sanchez — just wait on all those guys, and it might be two years, three years, four years before they all emerge? Or are we going to take the guys we have and try to move forward? Ultimately if you were going to try and move forward, there was a lot of work to do." With Reyes, Dickey, and Buehrle part of the core, there was less work for him to do for the 2014 season, though much of it required deft, nuanced touches.

Looking back, it may have been foolish to believe the Blue Jays could turn over half their roster and expect everything to come together in an instant. Eye-popping off-season buildups routinely fail in all professional sports — just look at the 2012–13 Los Angeles Lakers in the NBA, the 2012–13 Minnesota Wild in the NHL, or the 2012 Miami Marlins and 2011 Boston Red Sox in MLB. Winning the off-season guarantees nothing, and getting off on the right foot is so critical.

"It was a weird spring," says Anthopoulos. "We had more guys than anybody go to the World Baseball Classic. There was more media attention this spring than we had ever had. You've got a bunch of new star-calibre players coming together for the first time. It was just a really busy spring, new staff, new manager. The word new was all over the place."

Was too much new?

"It may have been," says Anthopoulos. "You wonder if we didn't have the Classic, does it change things. That's not an excuse, you just wonder. Everybody being together for a year, everybody being together all spring now, I expect there will be a lot less media attention on us next year. I think things will just stabilize and calm down quite a bit."

The way expectations upon the Blue Jays grew out of control may have been an albatross, too. From the moment the blockbuster with the Marlins was completed, a belief that a post-season berth was in the bag took hold. Fans believed. Pundits believed. Rival executives believed. Players believed. "Vegas had us winning it all," says Oliver, who put off retirement to take one final shot at winning a World Series. "God, man, what a turnaround it was."

At the first sign of trouble, hysteria instantly overtook reason, a constant for six months. Amplified by the power of social media, fans began to panic after the opening 2-4 homestand. The intense media focus meant players had to go out of their way to avoid hearing about the ongoing angst over what was wrong with the Blue Jays. After the opening-night loss, J.P. Arencibia quipped, "What's tough is we're not going to go undefeated this year. Going into it, I thought we had the chance to be the first 162-game winner." It was a clever remark, meant to invoke a touch of reality among excited fans, but also reflect a hyper-charged environment that not only created great expectations, but irrational ones.

"I think the more everyone was buying into what everyone else had to say about it, the harder we tried," says Lawrie. "I feel like all we had to do was do what we all needed to do individually, not go above and beyond what we were supposed to. When people were pushing the panic button, I think our team started to do that a little bit, and once that stopped, we all started to unwind a little bit." The experience was painful, but perhaps valuable as well, he adds. "It's a great learning season for our team, from the front office to the coaching staff to the players."

Dickey certainly concurs with the last part. "If we've gone through this year and we haven't grown at all by identifying what we've done poorly, then we're a failure."

The Toronto Blue Jays were a failure, an epic one, in 2013. Their redemption will come if, to borrow from Charles Dickens, they were bent and broken, but into a better shape.

*"Take nothing on its looks; take everything on evidence.
There's no better rule."*

—*Charles Dickens,*
Great Expectations

ACKNOWLEDGEMENTS

Taking on this project allowed us to delve into the stories of some truly remarkable people, along with the inner workings of a baseball team with so much on the line. We're grateful to publisher Jack David and ECW Press for presenting us with that opportunity, and for the work of the entire ECW team, especially Laura Pastore, our intrepid and meticulous editor, and managing editor Crissy Calhoun, for helping to pull the project together. We'd like to thank the dozens of Toronto Blue Jays players, coaches, executives and staffers, players and officials from other clubs, and everyone else who generously granted us their time and shared their insights. The cooperation of our employers, Sportsnet and the *National Post*, was instrumental in helping us to complete this project. We're grateful also to the Ontario Arts Council, whose support helped make this project possible. And to our loved ones, for their support, encouragement, and wise counsel, we couldn't have done it without you.

At ECW Press, we want you to enjoy this book in whatever format you like, whenever you like. Leave your print book at home and take the eBook to go! Purchase the print edition and receive the eBook free. Just send an email to ebook@ecwpress.com and include:

- the book title
- the name of the store where you purchased it
- your receipt number
- your preference of file type: PDF or ePub?

A real person will respond to your email with your eBook attached. And thanks for supporting an independently owned Canadian publisher with your purchase!

GET
THE
eBOOK
FREE

PROOF OF PURCHASE REQUIRED